THE BIBLE

A BEGINNER'S GUIDE TO STUDY AND UNDERSTAND SCRIPTURE

Edward Carbey

WHY YOU SHOULD READ THIS BOOK

This Project is to bring to the youngest minds- and not only them, but also interested adults- to the reading of the Bible through an agile and immediate reading.

Have this clear understanding that this is not a complete text, but an account of only the most significant facts in the history of Salvation, which always seek to place them in the global project of God. This is not written as replacement of the Bible, but an easy guide to the understanding of biblical stories through ages.

Read this Sacred book with due care. Not only will you find the historical manifestation of humanity and its interpretation with the eyes and heart of God, you will also find your story within the pages of this guide.

Enjoy the reading!

Table of Contents

INTRODUCTION TO THE BIBLE

Without gainsay in fact, the Bible is the most famous, most beautiful, and most important book in the world. The Bible narrates the history of salvation as the events chosen and performed by God to free humanity from evil and lead it to happiness. Men, from the very beginning of their appearance on earth, rebelled against their Creator; they turned away from Him. But God never ceased to love them. Even after their sin, they are not forgotten. He puts into effect a project to give humanity a future again, to rekindle hope in hearts, to restore lost happiness to men.

This project of God foresees many stages, and it is a progressive project. God cannot force men to approach him, love Him and love one another. God does not want to use coercion, but belief because he respects the freedom of his favorite creatures. God, with infinite patience, intends to educate men about love. By intervening in history, God wants to come and save men with their collaboration. Thus, this project of God, which will last centuries and centuries, is narrated in the Bible: the most famous, most beautiful and most outstanding guide in the world.

In truth, the Bible is not a single book; it is rather a collection of many books, some long, some very concise. They form like a small library, and it is precisely for this reason that the Bible is called that.

There are also many men who wrote the books of the Bible.

However, the true and only author of the Bible is **GOD** himself. In fact, not only did God choose and accomplish this project of salvation in the books of the Bible. Thus, men of all times could have known how much God did for their happiness, how much God loves them. In order for the authors of the books of the Bible to make no mistake in drafting the account of the project of salvation, God inspired them and assisted them as they wrote. They have therefore composed these books guided by God. Therefore the Bible is rightly called the Word of God. When you, therefore, read these pages, imagine that it is God who speaks to you. God wants you to understand just what you have done for your happiness, how much He loves you. God will also suggest how you must behave in order to be safe, to fully realize yourself, to be happy in this land and in the life that awaits you after death. God left the books of the Bible as a legacy, in his will, to the men of all times.

The Bible Is Divided Into Two Parts: The Old Testament And The New Testament.

The Old Testament tells the facts of salvation from the moment of the creation of the universe to the birth of Jesus. It includes 46 books, exposes the events that God has put in place to prepare humanity for the coming of Jesus, the true and only savior. It is Jesus who has brought us the forgiveness of the Father. It is Jesus who made us understand the love of the Father. To show us concretely and not only in words how much the Father loves us, but Jesus also died on the cross.

Jesus Begins New Humanity.

Jesus' death and his resurrection allow all men, if they wish, to dominate their passions and their low instincts, to overcome their selfishness, to overcome their anxieties and their fears. Jesus gave humanity a future, a hope. After Jesus, men know why they live and why they die. They know they have a Father who loves them. They know that the Father is waiting for them in his home to be happy, forever and forever.

The New Testament, which includes 27 books, tells the life, teaching, death and resurrection of Jesus and also the history of the early years of the church. The New Testament concludes with a book that explains what is yet to come: the last events of human history, the end of the world and the beginning of new life in the house of the Father for redeemed humanity.

The Bible, therefore, embraces the whole history of man, from creation to the end of time. Not all the facts of human history are told in the Bible, but only those that God has chosen and accomplished to bring men back to his love. The Bible narrates the 'facts' of salvation as they occur. So the Bible was written over a long period of time, almost a thousand years, from around 900 BC to about 100 AD. In this transcription of the Bible, only the most significant facts of the history of salvation are reported, trying to frame them always in the global project of God.

So read this holy book carefully. The Bible will teach you the way to go to God and the way to meet the brothers. Don't just learn the teachings the Bible offers you. He seeks above all to live them and to witness them every day before God and before men.

THE HISTORY OF ORIGINS
(GENESIS 1-11)

PART 1
THE EARTH AND THE UNIVERSE - THE WHY OF CREATION - THE DAYS OF CREATION

The earth and the universe

The earth is one of the nine planets in the solar system. The earth, which seems so big, is actually very small compared to the sun. If the earth is very small to the size of a pinhead, the proportional sun would be as big as a balloon and would be about seventy meters away. The sun with its planets is in turn part of an immense group of stars arranged in the shape of a disk. This cluster of stars forms the galaxy. The galaxy comprises about one hundred billion stars. Since there are about five billion men on earth, it can be said that every man has around twenty stars. The stars of the galaxy seem very close to each other. In reality, they are very far apart. The star closest to the sun is about four light years away. In other words, light takes about four years to cover this distance. The light moves at a very high speed: in one second it goes around the earth about seven times. The light takes about eight minutes to travel the distance between the sun and the earth. But the galaxy with its one hundred billion stars is not the whole universe. There are so many other galaxies in space, maybe a hundred billion, or even more. But at this point, not even the most fervent imagination can think of these magnitudes and distances.

Has the universe always been like this? Scientists today say that the universe is growing more and more like a rubber balloon that swells. About twenty billion years ago - say the scientists - this balloon was very small. Then suddenly a big explosion occurred. From that outbreak, the galaxies, the stars, the sun, the planets and even our earth were formed.

According to the scientists' calculations, the earth would be about four billion years old. On earth then life began much later. The man has finally appeared on the earth for a few million years. This is science. It intends to describe the facts as they occurred, but it does not explain why the facts were like this. Science does not explain the meaning of creation.

The reason for the creation

The Bible does not bother to explain how the universe, the earth and man came about. Rather, the Bible makes us understand the reason for creation. The biblical description of creation is not a scientific description. Moreover, the author of the creation story could not have known the laws of physics like today's scientists. The story of creation was written about three thousand years ago and then there were neither telescopes nor space probes. But the biblical creation story explains why the world exists and why man exists. The Bible explains the meaning of creation. The world and man exist because they were willed by God. God who is out of time because He is the Eternal that is to say, he has always existed, he wanted to give man existence. God is eternally happy and is happy to give. He wanted men to participate in his happiness. Thus God created the earth; this wonderful planet with its animals, plants, flowers, clouds, mountains, waters...

In this garden, God has placed his favorite creature, man. Man is the only being on earth capable of thinking, of wanting, of loving. As the Bible states, God created man in his image and likeness. Thinking, wanting and loving are specific activities of God. God created man to make him share in his own life. The life of God is a life of freedom, of love, of happiness.

The days of creation

"And God said, 'Let there be light,' and there was light." Gen. 1:3 (NIV)

The creation of the world and the creation of man are described in the first book of the Bible called Genesis, which means "origin". The facts of creation are not exposed by the Bible in scientific form. The Bible just wants us to understand that everything originated by the will of God and that God made everything good. The author of the creation story imagines that God accomplished his work in six days. *"Then God blessed the seventh day and made it holy because on it he rested from all the work of creating that he had done." (Gen. 2:3)* This is just a way of saying, it is a symbolic language. God is presented as a worker who works a week and then rests.

The scheme of the six days of work and the seventh day of rest was adopted by the author to teach men that they too must behave like God. Men must work, but they must also rest. Above all they must dedicate a day of the week to their Creator. They must offer God some of the time that God has given them. On the day of rest the men must take care of God, they must turn to him their thought and their prayer. In the Old Testament, the day of rest and prayer was Saturday. In the New Testament it is Sunday. The story of creation wants to remind us that one day in seven belongs totally to the Lord. We must not therefore think that the creation really took place in six days of twenty-four hours each and even in six years; it was millions of years long. The moments of creation were summarized in six days only to inculcate respect for work and rest in men.

"Now the earth was formless and empty, darkness was over the surface of the deep, and the Spirit of God was hovering over the waters." Gen. 2:3 (NIV)

The Bible imagines that chaos and disorder reigned at the beginning of time and therefore also of the universe. These expressions are equivalent to our "nothing". From this starting situation God has drawn the attention of the universe to putting order, dividing, and embellishing. God orders and adorns the world with his word. This way of expressing the Bible is also symbolic. In reality, God does not need to talk to do something. His thought is enough; an act of his will is enough. The will of God, when manifested, immediately produces facts always. Nothing can counteract God's will.

PART 2
EVERYTHING IS GOOD - ADAM AND EVE - THE FIRST HUMAN BEINGS

Everything is good

"God saw all that he had made, and it was very good. And there was evening, and there was morning the sixth day." Gen. 1:31

According to the weekly scheme, God creates light on the first day. This light is not the light of the sun because the sun, according to the same pattern, is created only on the fourth day. The ancient m en saw the light even when the sun had not yet risen, even when it was hidden by clouds, even when it had recently set. They, therefore, thought that light was a separate reality, independent of the sun. And God sees that light is a good thing. On the second day, God creates an immense vault, the firmament, to separate the waters that are above the sky from those that are under the sky. This description is also made according to the knowledge that the ancients had of the world. They thought that the earth was still and flat.

Above the earth, a transparent dome was stretched in the manner of a curtain to which the stars were attached. The sun, the moon and the planets also moved along the curve of the dome. Beyond the dome of the firmament lay the waters that men saw falling from the sky in the form of rain. The rain was possible - it was thought - because in the transparent vault of the firmament there were occasionally little windows or cataracts. On the third day, God gathers the lower waters and forms the oceans and the seas. God separates the earth from the waters. Then he adorns the dry earth of plants, each according to his own species. And God sees that everything is good. On the fourth day, God creates the sun, the moon and the stars. On the fifth day, God adorned the space between the earth and the vault of the sky with animals and adorned the waters of the oceans and seas with animals. Birds and fish appear each according to their species. And God sees that these animals are also good. On the sixth day, God fills the dry land with animals. Animals that jump, run, crawl, each according to its own species. Man appears on earth on the sixth day. On the seventh day, God rests. God blesses the seventh day and consecrates it, that is, establishes that that day is considered by all a sacred day.

Adam and Eve

"So the Lord God caused the man to fall into a deep sleep; and while he was sleeping, he took one of the man's ribs[g] and then closed up the place with flesh. Then the Lord God made a woman from the rib[h] he

had taken out of the man, and he brought her to the man." Gen. 2: 21-22

The creation of the woman is also told in the Bible in a symbolic way. To make us understand that man and woman have equal dignity, they are made of the same substance, they are a single reality, and the Bible says that God took the woman from a man's rib. The rib is the part of the body closest to the heart. The Bible with this expression means that man and woman were created by God to love each other, to be one heart, one flesh. The first two human beings that the Bible presents, Adam and Eve, represent all human beings in general wherever they appeared and whatever they looked like.

Also, the names that the Bible attributes to the first man and the first woman are symbolic. Adam means that he comes from the earth, which is made of earth. Eve means mother of the living. They are symbols and yet they are real because they really represent all the first human beings. Adam and Eve are not fictional, fictional characters. They have all the characteristics of the first human beings. Wherever they appeared and whatever they looked like, the first human beings behaved just like Adam and Eve. They rebelled against God after having been thought, loved, wanted and created by him.

The First Human Being

The first human beings, represented by Adam and Eve, live on earth substantially happy. The earth produces its fruits spontaneously. Men are few and there is plenty of food for everyone: it is enough to gather the fruits of the trees and the berries from the bushes.

The man has not yet become a farmer and does not need to cultivate the land to feed him. With his intelligence and his will, man becomes more and more evolved. He discovers and uses fire, works stone and builds tools, tames some species of animals and becomes a shepherd. In short, he lacks nothing to feel fully realized. Its basic needs can be met. Death itself is considered a natural fact that does not scare the man. He has a profound conviction that death is not the end of everything.

Primitive man considers the dead as living in another dimension, in a probably happier condition than that experienced on this earth. But above all the first men, represented by Adam and Eve before sin, are in harmony with themselves, with their fellows, with nature as a whole and in particular with animals. They feel protected, loved by their Creator.

PART 3
THE DEPENDENCE ON THE CREATOR - THE KNOWLEDGE OF GOOD AND EVIL - THE DISOBEDIENCE OF MAN

The dependence on the Creator

"Trust in the Lord with all your heart and lean not on your own understanding; in all your ways submit to him, and he will make your paths straight." Proverbs 3:5-6 (NIV)

However, man cannot consider himself the absolute master of creation or even the absolute master of himself. Man is still a limited creature, in need of so many things, a creature that depends, like all others, on the Creator. But unlike other living beings, which necessarily follow the laws of nature, man is free. God wanted the man responsible for his acts. Man can choose to do well or to do evil. Choosing good means doing what God has established for the happiness of man himself.

Man chooses happiness when he freely follows the laws that God has placed in his heart. Man must not kill his own kind, man must not hate, must not harm others in any way. Above all, man must respect God

15

and recognize him as his Creator. Not as a slave who obeys a master, but as a son who loves his father. Only by voluntarily obeying God can a man be fully realized, he can be happy.

The knowledge of good and evil

"The Lord God took the man and put him in the Garden of Eden to work it and take care of it. And the Lord God commanded the man, 'You are free to eat from any tree in the garden; but you must not eat from the tree of the knowledge of good and evil, for when you eat from it you will certainly die.'" Genesis 2:15-17 (NIV)

To describe the condition of the first men and their dependence on the Creator, the Bible still uses symbolic language. God - says the Bible - places man in a garden so that he can cultivate it and keep it. Then God gives the man this command: - You will be able to eat of all the trees of the garden, but of the tree of the knowledge of good and evil you must not eat, because, when you eat of it, you would certainly die.

With this prohibition, God wants to make the man understand that he must not consider himself the absolute master of everything. Man must recognize his own limits; he must accept the dependence on his Creator. The plant that the Bible calls "of the knowledge of good and evil" depicts the insurmountable limit of human freedom. Man is not free to decide what is good and what is bad. This

16

decision belongs only to God. In fact, only God can know what is good and what is bad for the man. God is the creator of man and only he knows what can benefit his creature and what can harm her. To eat the fruits of the plant of the knowledge of good and evil means to behave without taking into account the expressed will of God. A child cannot decide for himself what will do him good or what will damage him. God asks the man not to remain a child, but to trust him as a child trusts his mother and father.

Man's disobedience

*"For as by one man's disobedience many were made sinners, so by the obedience of one shall many be made righteous. "*Romans 5:19 (KJV)

Man is aware of his own limits. He understands that he cannot be an arbiter of himself or a judge of others. Man cannot do evil and then absolve himself. It cannot always be justified. However, man does not accept these conditionings. It does not take into account the prohibition of God to eat the fruits of the tree of the knowledge of good and evil. Man does not want to depend on God; he wants to plan for himself. It means the protection of God is a humiliation.

Before rebelling against God, man fights within himself. Doing without God in some ways scares him, for others, it fascinates him to rebel against God, become like him, is able to decide for oneself without laws, or be respected. The temptation to eat the forbidden fruits, to become the arbiter of one's actions, to establish for oneself what is good and what is bad is always stronger. It is as if someone inside the man suggests to him with a persuasive voice: *Take that fruit ... eat it ... you will become like God ... your eyes will finally open...*

These temptations that are within the heart of man are still described in the Bible with a symbolic language. The temptations are proposed to man by an animal that has always aroused in man certain disgust: the snake. The snake, slimy and sinuous, adored by some ancient peoples as a deity, represents for the Bible the spirit of evil, everything that is in some way opposed to God. The snake, the woman and the man. (Gen. 3:1-7) Each of the three protagonists has a share of responsibility in this sin of origins. The snake suggests for the woman to eat the forbidden fruit. The woman first promises the tempter the prohibition of God then lets her be convinced and bites the fruit.

Later, Adam is also dragged into sin. But the perspective presented by the snake is a deception. The first men immediately realize that without God one is ill. Without God we have confused ideas, we become enemies of other men. Sin is like going back, falling back into chaos, into disorder. Man is assailed by remorse. Sin weighs on his heart. The voice of his conscience condemns him.

18

PART 4
THE CONSEQUENCES OF SIN - FARMERS AND SHEPHERDS - CAIN AND ABEL

The consequences of sin

"For the wages of sin is death." Romans 6:23 (KJV)

After turning against God, the man realizes he has been deceived. Instead of feeling like God, he feels weak, unable to procure happiness alone. His low instincts dominate him. The image of God that man carried within himself seems to have blurred. His innocence, his joie de vivre, the harmonious relationship with nature, all this seems to have broken down. The man finds himself naked; he is ashamed of his own kind and covers the private parts of his body.

Man has interrupted communication with the Creator and becomes hostile towards his own kind. The man now fears pain and death. Death now seems the end of everything. There is no more hope for those who die. Man must work hard to live. The land that first produced its fruits spontaneously must now be processed. Man learns about agriculture. He must plough; sow if he wants to harvest.

*"To Adam, he said, 'Because you listened to your wife and ate fruit from the tree about which I commanded you, 'you must not eat from it,' 'Cursed is the ground because of you; through painful toil, you will eat food from it all the days of your life. It will produce thorns and thistles for you and you will eat the plants of the field. By the sweat of your brow, you will eat your food until you return to the ground since from it you were taken; for dust you are and to dust, you will return.'"*Genesis 3:17-19 (NIV)

This new condition of humanity is expressed in the Bible with a still symbolic story, but which summarizes and explains all the consequences of sin. Man feels accused by God and feels a great sense of guilt towards the Creator. He no longer addresses himself to him in prayer; rather he tries to hide, that is, to drive away God from his thoughts. But God seems to torment him deep in his conscience. Remorse eats man's heart.In vain he tries to discharge his guilt over the woman.

"Then the man said, 'The woman you put here with me—she gave me some fruit from the tree, and I ate it.' (Gen. 3:12). And in vain the woman, in turn, tries to put all the blame on the tempting snake. "Then the Lord God said to the woman, 'What is this you have done?' The woman said, 'the serpent deceived me, and I ate.' (3:13)

These attempts to discharge their responsibilities onto others demonstrate the lacerations that have occurred within man. By refusing dependence on the Creator, man has ruined himself with his own hands. He did not want to feel himself a child of God and became a slave to his own selfishness. But God does not abandon his favorite creature.

After having condemned men to labor fatigue (Gen. 3:17-19), having aroused that sense of guilt in their hearts, it promises salvation. He promises that evil will not have the final victory over good. Man will always be stronger than evil. One day, with God's help, man will definitively crush the head of the serpent, that is, evil will no longer harm man. Man will once again become the son of God. But first, the man will have to trudge up the slope of that ravine where sin has precipitated him. Man will have to learn to be more humble, to obey God, to trust him alone, to respect his law. God with infinite patience, because he is infinite love, he will renew man, he will bring him closer to himself, he will send the savior.

"For the Son of Man has come to seek and to save that which was lost." Luke 19:10 (NIV)

Immediately after the sin of the origins, God sets in motion a new project, a plan to recover lost humanity, meaningless and without a future. As a symbolic gesture of attention and love for sinful humanity, the Bible says that God, with fatherly tenderness, makes man and woman tunics of skins and dresses them. The salvation project involves long times. For the moment God wants to convince the man of the gravity of sin. It will take centuries and centuries for man to be persuaded that on his own he cannot make it, which on his own he cannot obtain happiness.

For the moment, he will have to suffer, struggle, die without hope. All this is described in the Bible with a truly terrifying and sad image for man. God drives out Adam and Eve from the garden where they were happy. Then God puts his angels in the guard of the garden with a dazzling sword in his hand.

"The Lord God made garments of skin for Adam and his wife and clothed them. And the Lord God said, 'The man has now become like one of us, knowing good and evil. He must not be allowed to reach out his hand and take also from the tree of life and eat, and live forever.' So the Lord God banished him from the Garden of Eden to work the ground from which he had been taken. After he drove the man out, he placed on the east side[e] of the Garden of Eden cherubim and a flaming sword flashing back and forth to guard the way to the tree of life." Genesis 3:21-24 (NIV)

Farmers and shepherds

"...Now Abel kept flocks, and Cain worked the soil." Genesis 4:2b

After the sin of pride committed by the first men, symbolically represented by Adam and Eve, humanity continues in its degradation. Sin against

God necessarily translates into sin against men. Men become violent. To survive they fight each other by killing each other. Enemies are killed and even the brothers are killed.

The man dedicates himself to agriculture and pastoral living to support him. Meanwhile, the first permanent settlements are being formed. The shepherd, forced to lead his flocks to the pastures, does not have a permanent home. He lives under the tent and is a nomad. When the grass dries in a pasture, the shepherd moves to greener areas.

The cultivators of the earth, on the other hand, build fixed, stone and brick dwellings. The first villages and the first cities rise. Farmers feel themselves to be masters of the land they cultivate. They harvest wheat and barley in the deposits. They do not fear the future because they have these provisions aside. They feel even more autonomous than God. The shepherd, on the other hand, has no land, no houses, and no provisions on the side. It has only the herd, often subject to disease and decimation due to lack of pastures. If it does not rain, the shepherd is lost.

The pastor feels more dependent on God. To propitiate God's favor, both pastors and farmers offer sacrifices. They warn God as a strict master and try to keep him good by burning a portion of the fruits of their labor on the altar. But the sacrifices of farmers are less spontaneous and sincere than those of shepherds. After all, farmers have their supplies; they can very well do without their protection and providence of God.

There are many tensions between farmers and shepherds and bloody clashes often take place: the former do not want the latter to pass with their flocks through the cultivated fields. The city, inhabited by farmers, and the steppe, where shepherds live, become irreconcilable enemies.

Cain and Abel

*"In the course of time, Cain brought some of the fruits of the soil as an offering to the Lord. And Abel also brought an offering—fat portions from some of the firstborn of his flock. The Lord looked with favor on Abel and his offering, but on Cain and his offering, he did not look with favor. So Cain was very angry, and his face was downcast."*Genesis 4: 3-5

This situation of rivalry and clash between the two ways of life is described in this chapter. Also, in this case, the Bible introduces two symbolic characters, two brothers, Cain and Abel who represent the two categories: farmers and shepherds. The two brothers make sacrifices to God, but God only likes those of Abel, the shepherd, because he finds them more sincere, more humble. Cain offers barley, wheat and fruit, but almost reluctantly. Abel offers the most tender and most beautiful lambs of his flock. Cain does not care too much about God's help. He also despises and envies his brother who considers him a loafer. A terrible passion creeps into Cain's heart: hatred of his brother. Cain is free and could overcome this passion. But he does not know how to dominate instinct, which like a beast crouches at the door of his heart.

Cain tells his brother one day, *"Let's go to the country." (Gen. 4:8)* While in the countryside, far from witnesses, Cain raises his hand against his brother Abel and kills him. It is the first crime described by the Bible, a murder that symbolizes all the violence of the bullies against the weak, *a horrendous* crime because every *man* is the brother of every other man. Even when a man kills a stranger or an enemy, he is like killing his own brother.

"Then the Lord said to Cain, "Where is your brother Abel?" "I don't know," he replied. "Am I my brother's keeper?" The Lord said, "What have you done? Listen! Your brother's blood cries out to me from the ground. Now you are under a curse and driven from the ground, which opened its mouth to receive your brother's blood from your hand. When you work the ground, it will no longer yield its crops for you. You will be a restless wanderer on the earth."Genesis 4:9-12 (KJV)

In the heart of Cain, though so harsh and cruel, remorse is immediately born, but Cain is proud. He doesn't admit he was wrong. And yet the blood of the murdered brother is always in front of him. He will no longer have peace of mind. He feels rejected by

God. His lands, his home, no longer give him security. He will go around the world looking for peace and trying to forget his grave crime. And once again God shows himself to be good and patient with the man.

God makes Cain feel remorse, but at the same time protects him from the vengeance of other men. God hates evil, does not want the man to be violent against his brother, but does not even want revenge. Even revenge, which seems justified by the offense received, it is evil before the eyes of God. Only God is the master of life and only God has the right to do justice. But God never revenges. God Forgives. When he punishes is not to take revenge, but to make the man understand his mistake because the man learns to behave like a brother with every other man.

PART 5

CONTINUOUS CORRUPTION - THE GREAT FLOOD - THE DESCENDANTS OF NOAH - THE TOWER OF BABEL

The corruption continues

"The Lord saw how great the wickedness of the human race had become on the earth, and that every inclination of the thoughts of the human heart was only evil all the time. The Lord regretted that he had made human beings on the earth, and his heart was deeply troubled. So the Lord said, 'I will wipe from the face of the earth the human race I have created— and with them the animals, the birds and the creatures that move along the ground—for I regret that I have made them. '"- Gen. 6:5-7

The inhabitants of the cities, those that the Bible calls the descendants of Cain, multiply above the earth and invent arts and crafts. The first musical instruments appear the zither, the flute. We learn the arts of spinning and weaving. Stone tools are abandoned and metal is worked. Even the art of the potter develops and the artifacts now have valuable forms. From prehistoric times humanity is turning to history.

Despite progress in all fields, man is always far from God. Violence, injustice, war, selfishness continue. Only a very small number of men honor God, offer sacrifices, and obey his law. The law of God is imprinted in the hearts of men, above all the law for the respect of life. But no one seems to care about the ban on killing. Only a few righteous people respect this law.

Among these righteous ones, there is one that the Bible presents as the new founder of humanity. The man is called Noah. (Gen. 6:8) He represents that part of humanity that had remained faithful to the Lord. The Noah clan lives in the Middle East, in a region called Mesopotamia which means "between two rivers". The two rivers that surround this region are the Tigris and the Euphrates. Often, after heavy rains, these rivers overflow and flood the entire inhabited area. God used one of these floods, during which there were hundreds or perhaps thousands of drowned people, to make the survivors understand the full gravity of their sins. This flood is remembered in the Bible as the universal flood.

The Great Flood (Genesis 6:9-7)

Thus, in Mesopotamia, Noah lives with his family. Noah has three children: Shem, Ham and Japheth. They are married and even Noah still has his wife. According to the Bible God turns to Noah to announce to him the punishment of the flood- the end of every man has come for me because the earth is full of violence because of them.

God then suggests to Noah a way to save himself from the terrible flood: he teaches him to build an ark, a kind of houseboat. The ark is 156 meters long, 26 meters wide and 15 meters high. (Gen. 6:14-17) These measures seem the most suitable for dealing with flood waves and vortices. God forces Noah to carry every species of animal from that area of the earth with him to the ark, especially domestic animals, one of the main resources of the time.

"The Lord then said to Noah, 'Go into the ark, you and your whole family, because I have found you righteous in this generation. Take with you seven pairs of every kind of clean animal, a male and its mate, and one pair of every kind of unclean animal, a male and its mate, and also seven pairs of every kind of bird, male and female, to keep their various kinds alive throughout the earth. Seven days from now I will send rain on the earth for forty days and forty nights, and I will wipe from the face of the earth every living creature I have made."- Gen. 7:1-4 (NIV)

After the flood the earth would have been covered with mud and for many years could not have sustained the man. Noah faithfully carries out the orders of the Lord and, amid the scornful laughter of his neighbors, prepares with his sons to build this immense floating house. The work takes a long time, but finally the big boat is ready. Noah goes up there with his children, his wife, his daughters-in-law and a couple of animals to save. The ark is supplied with adequate provisions. And immediately begins a thick and incessant rain that lasts many days, always the same, and obsessive.

"And Noah and his sons and his wife and his sons' wives entered the ark to escape the waters of the flood. Pairs of clean and unclean animals, of birds and of all creatures that move along the ground, male and female, came to Noah and entered the ark, as God had commanded Noah. And after the seven days the floodwaters came on the earth."
(7:7-10)

The small windows or cataracts placed, according to the mentality of the time; on the vault of the sky seem to have all been wide open and forever. Indeed it seems that the entire vault of the firmament has collapsed and that all the upper waters are pouring over the earth. The Tigris and the Euphrates overflow overwhelming homes and entire villages. The ark rose by the water floats and Noah can save himself with his family. The ark is transported far away and finally settles on land.

Noah after making sure that there is no longer any danger, he comes out of the ark to thank the Lord with a sacrifice. (Gen. 8:20) A beautiful rainbow shines in the sky. The men already knew the rainbow arch that looks like a bridge thrown between the earth and the sky. But this time the rainbow takes on a very special meaning. The rainbow looks like an architectural element that supports the vault of the sky reinforcing it, closing cataracts, dividing the waters above it from those on the earth. The rainbow is the sign that God will no longer allow the upper waters to mix ruinously with the lower ones. The rainbow is the joyful and sure proof that God made peace with the new humanity represented by Noah and his sons. (9:12-13)

The whole earth looks as fresh and innocent as the first day of creation. God renews the command to Noah to respect the lives of other men and promises his blessing and protection in return. A covenant is established between God and Noah. If Noah and his descendants will respect life and no longer use violence, God will never again punish humanity.

" '...Whenever I bring clouds over the earth and the rainbow appears in the clouds, 15 I will remember my covenant between me and you and all living creatures of every kind. Never again will the waters become a flood to destroy all life. 16 Whenever the rainbow appears in the clouds, I will see it and remember the everlasting covenant between God and all living creatures of every kind on the earth. '"-Gen. 9:14-16 (NIV)

After the flood, it's as if human history begins again. God, after the failure of Adam and his descendants, recreated new humanity more obedient to him, more respectful of his will.

The descendants of Noah

Unfortunately, even this "second humanity" fails. Already one of the sons of Noah, Ham, behaves in a very disrespectful way towards his old father. *"Ham, the father of Canaan, saw his father naked and told his two brothers outside."* *(Gen. 9:22)* After the flood, Noah and his sons resume cultivating the land.

At that time the vine plant was discovered. Men learn to prepare wine by crushing grapes and fermenting the must. Probably the first times they drink grape juice they don't realize its possible intoxicating effects. So it happens to Noah. After drinking an abundant dose of wine to quench his thirst, Noah falls asleep inside his tent. Half naked and thrown on the ground, it certainly does not offer an edifying spectacle! *(Gen. 9:20)* Ham accidentally enters the tent and sees his father in that state. Immediately he begins to laugh. Then he goes out to invite the brothers to enjoy that scene.

Shem and Japheth severely reproach Ham. Then they take a cloak and, walking backwards so as not to see their sprawled father, cover it with much respect. When Noah wakes up, he curses Cam for his foolishness and offers him a future full of pain and difficulty.

"When Noah awoke from his wine and found out what his youngest son had done to him, he said, 'Cursed be Canaan! The lowest of slaves will he be to his brothers.'" (Gen. 9:24-25)

Instead, he blesses Shem and Japheth for the respect they have shown him. *(Gen. 9:26-27)*

Once again humanity is thus divided into good and bad. It seems that the lesson of the flood was not enough to direct men towards the good, towards respect for others. Years pass. Mankind has now spread throughout the then known land. There are now many peoples, but everyone still speaks a language that has a common origin. But soon men, for a new sin of pride, will no longer keep even this last sign of unity.

The Tower of Babel

The cities that the descendants of Noah build along the rivers of Mesopotamia become increasingly large, populous, and splendid. The architecture has developed and now the buildings rise boldly towards the sky. In particular, along the Euphrates River, a beautiful and very rich city is rising: Babylon.

Inside its walls, superb pyramids made in steps rise up, which seem, also due to their shape, immense stairs that rise towards the abode of the gods. Corruption also grows in Babylon with wealth and power. Men, forgetful of the one true God, worship absurd and cruel idols made of stone. They even offer human sacrifices to them.

The Bible takes its cue from the memory of one of these pyramids remained unfinished, to describe in the eleventh chapter of Genesis, the pride of men and the consequent punishment of God. The inhabitants of Babylon, therefore, say to each other, *"Come, let us do bricks and cook them on the fire. Let us build a tower whose top touches the sky."* (Gen. 11:1-9) But the Lord punishes their presumption. Man can build nothing important if he forgets God or, worse, defies God. The pyramid is not completed because men begin to quarrel among themselves. It is as if God has confused their languages so that they no longer understand each other.

In reality, the multiplication of languages was a natural phenomenon, due to the continuous shifting of those populations. But certainly, the dispersion of peoples also means the will of men not to cooperate with each other, to act according to their own interests. A new negative experience of humanity is a further occasion for the Bible to teach men that civilization cannot be built without God.

With the experience of the Tower of Babel, it now seems that God, impatient with the proud behaviour of men, must abandon them to their fate. It seems that the plan to recover sinful humanity has definitively failed.

God instead starts all over again. Once again his love is stronger than human pride. God will choose a new man to make him the forefather of a new humanity. This man will be Abraham and from his descendants, God will give birth to the saviour. The first eleven chapters of Genesis tells the story of the origins of humanity, a story that covers a very long period, lasted millennia and millennia, a period during which men had not yet invented writing, a period therefore very difficult to reconstruct historically. With Abraham, however, we are already entering history. Abraham, who lived around 1800/1700 BC, is the first historical character that the Bible presents to us.

THE HISTORY OF THE PATRIARCHES
(Genesis 12-50)

PART 1
THE CLAN OF THE SEMITES - THE CLAN OF ABRAHAM - THE VOCATION OF ABRAHAM - THE COVENANT BETWEEN GOD AND ABRAHAM

The clan of the Semites

Abraham is a descendant of Shem, one of the sons of Noah; therefore he is of Semite lineage. Semites do not live in cities but are semi-nomadic shepherds. They move seasonally with their flocks of sheep and goats. When the rains make the grass grow in the steppes, the shepherds bring the flocks to them and then return, during the months of drought, to the places where they normally live. When they are not in the pastures they pitch tents along the banks of the Euphrates River.

The Semites do not participate in the life of large cities like Babylon. They are free and are organized in very large families. The forefather governs the family and is usually a wise old man, a patriarch, a leader to whom children with wives and children of children blindly obey. These families or clans can include dozens and dozens of members without counting servitude.

The Semitic clans, in particular circumstances, come together: to face, for example, long or difficult journeys or to defend themselves against common enemies. Very strict laws apply in the clan. The patriarch is the supreme authority: he is a father, judge and priest at the same time. Before dying, the patriarch transmits his authority to his firstborn son. All wealth is transferred together with authority. In addition, the patriarch gives his son a personal blessing with the guarantee of future prosperity.

The clan of Abraham

At the head of Abraham's clan is the wise old Terah. He has three sons: Abraham, the firstborn, and then Nahor and Haran. Terah and the members of his clan do not know the true God. They honour domestic deities that are depicted as small human figures shaped with clay. When the clan moves with the flocks, it also carries these protective deities.

Around the year *1750 BC*, the Babylonian emperor Hammurabi attempts the creation of a powerful and unified empire. He tries to subdue all the populations of the region, including the clans of the Semitic shepherds. The Terah clan that is expected at the city of Ur south of Babylon, jealous of its traditions and freedom, decides to move further north. The migration takes place along the "fertile crescent", a strip of land that, from the Mesopotamia, describing a wide arc, reaches the mouth of The Nile.

One day, therefore, old Terah, with the children and children of his sons and servants and flocks, raises the curtains and moves north. After many days of walking the clan reaches the city of Harran and waits nearby. Abraham, the firstborn, is married like his brothers, but unlike these, he has no children. Abraham is no longer so young. Even Sara, his bride, is old and can no longer have children. Abraham will therefore not inherit the authority of the father, will not receive the riches, and will not have the blessing. Abraham is without descendants and therefore without a future.

But precisely because he is without a future, he is elected by God to be the forefather of the new humanity, the founder of a people from whom the saviour would have risen. By choosing Abraham, God wants to show that salvation does not come through human means, but only for his power and his mercy.

The vocation of Abraham

Abraham watches his father's flock near the city of Harran in the long starry nights. While the animals rest, old Abraham reflects on his future. It's so sad. *"I'm approaching the grave - think old Abraham - and I have no children. My life was useless...."* Abraham looks at the stars of heaven.

39

They are as numerous as the sand grains of the desert. Inside the tent, Sara rests quietly. And here, in the silence of the night, Abraham hears a mysterious voice, firm and at the same time very sweet. It seems to come from the immensity of the sky or perhaps the wind brought it from those sand dunes there or perhaps it comes from the depths of Abraham's soul.

The voice says, "Abraham, leave this country, from the house of your father. Go to the country that I will show you. I will make you great people and I will bless you. I will make your name great. I will bless those who bless you and those who curse you I will curse. All the families of the earth will be blessed in you." (Gen. 12:1-3) Abraham does not immediately understand the meaning of these words. But he trusts that voice. On those promises, he will found his future. He will have no other security.

Thinking back to those words, Abraham is convinced that they come from God, the true and only God, an infinite being like the sky, as immense as the desert and yet close as a friend and Provident as a father and tender as a mother. Abraham believes this God, his God. He entrusts his own existence to him without asking questions or setting conditions. Now he is no longer sad, he is no longer afraid of the future, he has no more doubts.

"So Abram went, as the Lord had told him; and Lot went with him. Abram was seventy-five years old when he set out from Harran. He took his wife Sarai,

his nephew Lot, all the possessions they had accumulated and the people they had acquired in Harran, and they set out for the land of Canaan, and they arrived there." (Gen. 12:4-5)

The next morning Abraham with his wife Sarah and with Lot, son of his brother Aran, leave Harran. Both Abraham and A lot lead their flocks. They head south to the land of Canaan. Abraham is 75 years old when he leaves his father's house. He knows that God's promises are in contrast with reality, with logic. Yet he leaves with the certainty in his heart. God, his God, will not deceive him, he will not disappoint him. The promises will come true because God is faithful. Abraham, after many days of travel, arrives in the country of Canaan, or Palestine. He stops in the town of Shechem. (Gen. 12:6-9). Here he still hears the mysterious, firm and very sweet voice: To your descendants - God promises - I will give this country.

The covenant between God and Abraham

From the land of Canaan, Abraham proceeds along the Fertile Crescent to Egypt. He cannot stay anywhere because he is in a foreign land. Abraham does not care to know when God will keep his promises. He lives in temporariness, letting himself be guided from time to time by that mysterious voice. He does not even know the name of the God who speaks to him. Abraham calls him El, which perhaps

41

means "That". A generic name, but which contains all the mystery and transcendence of divinity.

"So Abram said to Lot, 'Let's not have any quarreling between you and me, or between your herders and mine, for we are close relatives. Is not the whole land before you? Let's part company. If you go to the left, I'll go to the right; if you go to the right, I'll go to the left.'"- Gen. 13:8-9

Returning from Egypt, Abraham pitches his tents at Bethel in Canaan. There Abraham separates himself from Lot. The grandson, with a part of the flocks, goes along the valley of the Jordan River towards the cities of Sodom and Gomorrah. Abraham instead settles at Bethel. And here, once again, the voice of God makes itself heard to the old pastor,

"I am your shield," says God. "Your reward will be very large." Abraham answers, "My Lord, what will you give me? I go to the grave without children. You didn't give me descendants." And the voice said, "Look at the sky and count the stars if you can count them. This will be your descendants. I will also give you this country." And Abraham replied, "Lord my God, how will I know that I will have possession?" The voice said, "Take a three-year-old heifer, a three-year-old goat, a three-year-old ram, a turtle-dove and a pigeon. Divide them into two and place each half in front of the other." (Gen. 13:14-17)

With these words, God proposes to Abraham a kind of oath. This ritual was practised when the leaders of two clans exchanged promises or made an alliance to face a common enemy. The leaders of the two clans, after having arranged the divided animals in a row, passed among them. This passage meant that if one of the two contractors had not kept the promises of mutual help, he would have suffered the same fate as the quartered animals.

This same oath God proposes to Abraham as if to reassure him that he would keep his promises to grant him descendants and land. So Abraham takes the animals, squares them and arranges them in a row.

As the sun is about to set, a numbness falls on Abraham. Then it gets dark after the sun has set. And here a globe of fire passes among the divided animals. That fire represents God himself. Passing among the animals, God solemnly swears to Abraham to keep his promises. Only God passes as if to signify that the initiative of that alliance is his alone.

That covenant, rather than a pact between two persons of equal dignity, is a free gift that comes from the love and benevolence of God. To Abraham God asks only unlimited trust and absolute obedience. As an external sign of these dispositions, God asks Abraham that all the male children of his future descendants be circumcised. Circumcision was a practice already used by some ancient peoples. It consisted of an incision of the skin in the male member.

" 'For the generations to come every male among you who is eight days old must be circumcised, including those born in your household or bought with money from a foreigner—those who are not your offspring. Whether born in your household or bought with your money, they must be circumcised. My covenant in your flesh is to be an everlasting covenant. Any uncircumcised male, who has not been circumcised in the flesh, will be cut off from his people; he has broken my covenant. ' " – Gen. 17:12-14

God imposes this practice on Abraham as if to remind him that every child was considered a gift.

PART 2
THE SON OF THE PROMISE - THE DESTRUCTION OF SODOM AND GOMORRAH - THE BIRTH AND SACRIFICE OF ISAAC - ISAAC'S MARRIAGE

The son of promise

"Then God said, "Yes, but your wife Sarah will bear you a son, and you will call him Isaac. I will establish my covenant with him as an everlasting covenant for his descendants after him. And as for Ishmael, I have heard you: I will surely bless him; I will make him fruitful and will greatly increase his numbers. He will be the father of twelve rulers, and I will make him into a great nation. But my covenant I will establish with Isaac, whom Sarah will bear to you by this time next year." When he had finished speaking with Abraham, God went up from him." – Gen. 17:19-22

After the alliance, some time passes. Abraham firmly continues to believe that God will finally give him an heir. But Sara, his wife, cannot conceive. Humiliated for her sterility, she then makes a proposal to her husband,

"Behold, the Lord prevents me from having offspring. Join my slave, Agar. You can have a child with her. Perhaps this is the meaning of the promise God has given you."

Abraham listens to Sara's suggestion. Hagar gives birth to a son, Ishmael, which means *"God hears"*. But this is not the meaning of the promise made by God. The people that God wants cannot descend from a slave

One evening Abraham is sitting at the entrance of his tent planted near some oak trees in the town of Mamre. And here are three men approaching him. (Gen. 18:1-13) Immediately Abraham goes to meet them, "Sit down under these oaks," he tells them full of solicitude. *"Allow me to go and get a bite of bread. Rest, you will be tired. Then you can continue."* Abraham hurries into the tent and tells Sara, "Quickly, knead a little flour and make cakes."

Then he runs to the herd, takes a tender and good calf and hands it to a servant to prepare it for a feast. Finally, he offers bowls of fresh milk to the three mysterious guests. The three refresh themselves, and then the one who seems the most authoritative asks Abraham, *"Where is Sarah, your wife?"* Abraham replies, "inside the tent."

Then that mysterious and authoritative man says to Abraham, *"In a year, I will return to you and then Sara will have a son."* Sara in the tent hears those words and immediately bursts into disbelief in laughter. And the man says, *"Why did Sara laugh? Is there something impossible for the Lord?"* And his voice is firm and sweet. The same voice had already spoken to Abraham in the city of Harran, near the town of Shechem and near the town of Bethel.

Then the three get up and move towards the cities of Sodom and Gomorrah. Abraham accompanies them, according to the duties of hospitality, for a stretch of road.

The destruction of Sodom and Gomorrah

"Then the Lord rained down burning sulfur on Sodom and Gomorrah—from the Lord out of the heavens. Thus he overthrew those cities and the entire plain, destroying all those living in the cities— and also the vegetation in the land. But Lot's wife looked back, and she became a pillar of salt." – Gen.19:24-26

While Abraham and his guests walk towards Sodom, the most authoritative of the three says, *"I am going to destroy Sodom and Gomorrah because the corruption of those two cities is great."* His voice that used to be firm and sweet is now veiled with sadness. Abraham says,

"Will you really exterminate the just along with the wicked? If there were fifty righteous people in the city, do you really want to suppress them?" *"If I find fifty righteous ones in Sodom," says the guest, "I will forgive the whole city for their sake."*

Abraham starts talking again and says, "Perhaps the fifty righteous will miss five. Will you destroy the whole city for these five?" "I won't do it!"

Abraham still intercedes for the two corrupt cities. But not even ten just live within the walls of Sodom. Lot, Abraham's nephew, and his family had also settled in Sodom. The three mysterious characters come to the city, while Abraham returns to his tent. Lot, his wife and children are upright people and have never approved the corruption of the inhabitants of Sodom. Therefore the three characters tell Lot

, "We are about to destroy this place. But you, with your family, leave the city because we don't want to overwhelm you in the punishment. Don't look back, though, and don't stop until you are away, safe."(Gen. 19:17)

Lot and his family run the council of the three and quickly move away from Sodom.

The sun has just risen on the horizon when the Lord rains sulfur and fire from the sky above Sodom and Gomorrah. The Lord destroys the cities and the valley with all the inhabitants and the vegetation of the soil. Lot's wife who, in the glow of the fire, turns back, remains electrocuted.

Abraham goes to the place of destruction early in the morning and contemplates the expanse of the valley from above. He sees the smoke rising from the earth and it is like the smoke of a furnace. Abraham understands that the God of promise is also a terrible God, a God who cannot stand evil. Abraham understands that God if he punishes men, He does that to tear them from evil. Punishment seems to be the only way left to God to make people understand that they must reject evil and choose well. Abraham understands that when God punishes, his heart is full of sadness.

The birth and sacrifice of Isaac

"Sarah said, 'God has brought me laughter, and everyone who hears about this will laugh with me.'"- Gen. 21:6

Before the year expires, according to the promise of Abraham's guest to the oaks of Mamre, Sarah gives birth to a son. Abraham calls Isaac the son of the promise. Then he circumcised him as God had commanded him and meanwhile he said to himself, *"Who would have said to Abraham: Sarah must nurse children! Yet she gave birth to a child in her old age!" (21:7)* Soon rivalry arises among the slave Hagar who had given Abraham a son, Ishmael, and Sarah who now also has a son. Abraham is then forced to remove Hagar and Ishmael from his tent. But God does not abandon the slave and his young son and from Ishmael, he will bring down the great and noble people of the Arabs. *(Genesis 21:11-21)*

Meanwhile, Isaac grows handsome and robust under the smug gaze of his old parents. But the trials for

Abraham has not ended. God wants to strengthen the faith and obedience of the one who was to become the forefather of the chosen people.

One day Abraham still hears the mysterious, firm and sweet voice that calls him, *"Abraham, Abraham!"* *"Here I am!"* The old patriarch responds promptly. The voice resumes, *"Take your son, your only son, you love and offer him as a burnt offering on a mountain that I will show you."* *(Gen. 22:2)*

The Holocaust consisted of sacrificing the victim by slaughtering it, bleeding it and then burning it completely over the altar. Abraham, hearing this command of the Lord, feels lost. Hadn't he promised him that sweet and terrible God who would be born from Isaac numerous people like the stars? And now that same God, contradicting himself, orders him to kill the son of the promise!

But Abraham, in his unshakable faith, makes no objection. He obeys the Lord even if the command is against logic, against reason, against the very voice of blood. Abraham gets up early in the morning, saddles the donkey, picks up the wood and then starts with his son Isaac towards the place God has shown him. During the journey, Isaac asks his father, *"Father, here is wood for the fire, but where is the lamb for the holocaust?"* *(22:7)* Abraham with his heart beating fast, overcoming emotion, replies, *"God himself will provide the lamb for the holocaust, my son."* They arrived on the mountain and prepared the altar. Abraham without hesitation is about to dip the long knife in Isaac's throat, when the mysterious voice, firm and very sweet, tells him,

"Abraham, Abraham, do not stretch out your hand against the boy and do no evil. Now I know you fear God and you have not refused your child, your only son."

Then Abraham, with his heart lifted by the mortal anguish that had accompanied him throughout the journey, looks up. Entangled with horns in a bush, he sees a ram struggling. He understands that this is the victim the Lord wants in a holocaust. And the voice says to Abraham: "Because you have not refused me your son, I will bless you with every blessing and I will make your descendants as numerous as the stars of the sky and like the sand that is on the shore of the sea.

Isaac's marriage

"'Here is Rebekah; take her and go, and let her become the wife of your master's son, as the Lord has directed.'" – Genesis 24:51

Isaac grows beautiful and vigorous next to his old parents. He too, like his father and his father's father, is a shepherd. Leads the flocks and herds along the gentle hills of the land of Canaan. Abraham's brother, Nahor, remained in the city of Harran where the tomb of Father Terah was. Nahor had children and children from his children. His last son, Bethuel, had a daughter named Rebecca about the same age as Isaac. Rebecca is a gorgeous, dark and slender girl. Abraham is very old and will soon go down to the grave as his father and his father's father.

Sara is already dead and Abraham to bury her worthily bought a small piece of land at the Machpelah Cave. That land bought by Abraham is the first property of the old patriarch. Until then he had lived without even possessing a cloud of that land promised to his descendants.

So, one day Abraham, feeling himself close to death, wants to marry his son Isaac to secure the lineage promised by God. According to the customs of Jewish shepherds, marriages had to take place among the members of the same clan. Abraham had heard that his brother Nahor had children and grandchildren. Therefore he sends a servant to the city of Harran to choose a wife for his son Isaac from the descendants of Nahor. The servant leaves and arrives at the city. He stops beside a well to water his camels. And here comes out of the city a group of young girls who come to the well to draw water. The servant says to him,

"She, who will give me and my camels to drink, will be the bride whom the Lord has chosen for Isaac."

As soon as one of the maidens, a splendid, slender, dark girl, filled the amphora, the servant asks her to drink, *"Drink, my lord,"* replies the girl. ***"Indeed I will draw water even for your camels."*** The servant asks her, ***"Who are you? Whose daughter are you?"*** ***"I am Rebecca, daughter of Bethuel, son of Nahor,"*** the girl replies.

The servant understands that this is the bride God chose for Isaac and accompanies the girl from Abraham. Isaac and Rebecca get married. Abraham blesses his son and leaves him heir to the promises of God. After a short time, he dies. Isaac buries him in the cave of Machpelah, next to his wife Sara.

PART 3
ESAU SELLS THE BIRTHRIGHT - ISAAC'S BLESSING - JACOB'S DREAM - JACOB'S TWO MARRIAGES

Esau sells the birthright

"Once when Jacob was cooking some stew, Esau came in from the open country, famished. He said to Jacob, "Quick, let me have some of that red stew! I'm famished!" (That is why he was also called Edom. Jacob replied, "First sell me your birthright. Look, I am about to die," Esau said. "What good is the birthright to me?" But Jacob said, "Swear to me first." So he swore an oath to him, selling his birthright to Jacob. Then Jacob gave Esau some bread and some lentil stew. He ate and drank, and then got up and left. So Esau despised his birthright."
– Genesis 25:29-34

Isaac, after his father's death, becomes the head of the clan. His wife Rebecca has two twin sons. The first to be born is Esau and, immediately afterwards, Jacob sees the light. The inheritance and blessing of Isaac would, therefore, be touched by Esau, according to the law of primogeniture.

The years go by. Esau is now a tall and strong young man like an oak. His body is covered with thick reddish hair. Jacob, on the other hand, is thin and sweet in character. Esau is a skilled hunter, while Jacob prefers to stay in the tent to keep his mother company.

One day Jacob cooked lentil soup. Esau comes from tired and hungry countryside. He tells his brother, *"Let me eat some of this soup, because I'm exhausted."* Jacob takes advantage of the circumstance. He cared about his birthright. He ardently desired to receive Isaac's blessing. Then he says to his brother: "I'll give you this soup if you give me your birthright right away." Esau replies: - Here, I'm starving. What then is the birthright for me? Esau sells his right under oath to his twin brother for a plate of lentil soup. Certainly, Jacob proves himself a profiteer on this occasion. But, between the two brothers, Esau behaves worse. At this point he despises his father's blessing, to be swapped for a plate of soup! At least Jacob proves to appreciate the blessing even if he uses blackmail to get it.

Isaac's blessing

" 'Prepare me the kind of tasty food I like and bring it to me to eat, so that I may give you my blessing before I die.' "- Genesis 27:4

Years and years still pass. Isaac is old now and his eyes are so weak that he can't see us anymore. He too, like his father Abraham, feeling close to death, intends to pass on to his eldest son, Esau the blessing that contains God's promise of land and of numerous descendants like the stars. Isaac ignores the fact that Esau, many years before, sold his birthright to his brother Jacob. Even Esau probably forgot about that lentil soup. Jacob, on the other hand, has not forgotten that, according to his mother Rebecca. He has always wanted Isaac's blessing and inheritance.

One day old Isaac calls the eldest son Esau and tells him, "My son, see, I am old. Take your weapons, your quiver and your bow, go out into the countryside and capture game for me. Then prepare me a dish of my taste and bring me food, because I [would like to] bless you before I die." While Isaac speaks to his son, Rebecca listens in secret. Esau goes hunting for safe and bold game. Meanwhile Rebecca tells her son Jacob, "Soon, go to the flock and take two tender kids. I'll make a dish for your father. You will bring it to him and he will bless you." Jacob timidly objects to his mother, saying "Esau is hairy while I have smooth skin. Perhaps my father will touch me and notice the deception [in this scheme of ours] and I will attract a curse instead of a blessing." Rebecca cuts him short, "You obey and go get the kids. I'll take care of the rest." Rebecca takes Esau's clothes and has them worn by Jacob; then, with the skins of the two kids, he covers the arms and neck of the favourite son.

When Jacob presents himself to the old and blind Isaac, he tells him, *"How quickly did you find and cook the game, my son? Get closer and let me bless you to know if you're really my son Esau."* Jacob approaches trembling to his old father. Isaac touches him on the arms and on the neck then says, *"Reassured, the voice is that of Jacob, but the arms are the arms of Esau."* Isaac still inhales the smell of the clothes that Jacob wears, and then says,

> *"The smell of my son is like the smell of a field that the Lord has blessed. God grant you fat lands and an abundance of wheat and must. The people [shall] serve you and the people [shall] prostrate themselves before you. I bless you and who blesses you is blessed and who curses you is cursed."*
> *Genesis 27:27-29*

Isaac has just finished speaking when Esau comes from hunting with the game for his father. But it's too late. The blessing, once given, could no longer be withdrawn. Esau does not forgive his brother for this deception and seeks revenge. He wants to kill his brother.

Rebecca then advises Jacob, *"Soon, you [should] flee to the city of Harran and take refuge with my brother Laban."* So, first with blackmail and then with deception, Jacob becomes the new head of the clan and inherits the promise made by God to Abraham. God, accepting Jacob's not too clear action, wants to show that his project of salvation is entrusted to those who appreciate it and not to those who rely only on their own human rights. Salvation is a gift and like all gifts, it is offered to those who know how to receive it.

Jacob's dream

"He [Jacob] had a dream in which he saw a stairway resting on the earth, with its top reaching to heaven, and the angels of God were ascending and descending on it." – Genesis 28:12

Jacob, in order to escape his brother's vengeance departs following his mother's advice and heads for the town of Harran to the north.

One evening he arrives in a lonely place and is about to spend the night there. He takes a flat stone, places it like a pillow, lies down and falls asleep. During that night Jacob makes a strange dream. A ladder is resting on the ground, while its top reaches the sky. And here are the angels that rise and fall upon it.

Always in the dream, Jacob feels a firm and sweet voice, "I am the God of Abraham and the God of Isaac, your father. The earth on which you lay down I will give to you and your descendants. Your descendants will be as numerous as the grains of dust on the earth. And all nations will be blessed through you and your descendants. I am with you and I will protect you wherever you go."- Genesis 28:13-15

When Jacob wakes up the next morning, remembering his dream, he understands that God has confirmed the blessing of old Isaac. The earth and the sky, united by a ladder, I agree. Jacob is the sure heir of God's promise to Abraham. The saviour of all humanity will come from his descendants.

To celebrate that event Jacob sets up the stone used during the night for a pillow, and calls that lonely place *Bethel*, which means *"House of God"*.

Jacob's two marriages

"And Jacob did so. He finished the week with Leah, and then Laban gave him his daughter Rachel to be his wife."- Genesis 29:28

Jacob, comforted by the dream, sets off again heading towards the city of Harran. Before entering the city, tired and thirsty, he stopped to drink near the well where his mother Rebecca was already coming to draw water. At that moment a beautiful girl named Rachael, daughter of Laban, Rebecca's brother arrives at the well. Rachel is Jacob's cousin.

The young man reveals himself to Rachel, who immediately runs to report the meeting to his father. Laban immediately goes out to meet Jacob, kisses him and leads him to his home. Laban has another daughter, Leah, a few years older than the beautiful Rachael. But Leah isn't as pretty as her sister.

Jacob fell in love with Rachael the moment he met her at the well. He, therefore, asked his uncle Laban for permission to take her as a wife. Laban, who is even more astute than Jacob himself, thinks he is exploiting the situation. He promises Rachael to his grandson in love on condition that he works for him for at least seven years. (Genesis 29:20) Jacob, in order to have Rachael, consents and serves the uncle for seven interminable years.

When he finally reaches the longed-for wedding day, Laban grants Jacob not Rachael, but the other daughter Leah. In fact, he wanted first to marry his eldest daughter, who otherwise, as plain as she was, would not have easily found a husband. **(29:22)** Jacob obviously gets upset, but his intention to marry Rachael does not change. **(29:25**)

However, to grant Jacob also Rachael, Laban demands that the young man serve him for another seven years. Thus Jacob, after fourteen years of almost forced labour, now finds himself a mature man with two wives.

At that time, having more than one wife was quite normal. All the peoples of the Middle East practised polygamy. God, in carrying out his project of salvation, often adapts to the customs of the times because he wants to educate his people gradually.

Later God will ask to abandon polygamy, and with Jesus, he will teach that marriage is a sacred fact, a sacrament. For the moment Jacob has to take the two sisters home. In time he will even be able to love Leah, the dull-eyed wife. From the two wives and also from some slaves, Jacob will have twelve sons: Reuben, Simeon, Levi, Judah, Issachar, Zebulun, Dan, Naphtali, Gad, Asher, Joseph, and Benjamin. Only the last two are sons of Rachel and are those that Jacob will love more than others.

PART 4
JACOB RETURNS TO CANAAN - JACOB STRUGGLES WITH GOD - THE MEETING BETWEEN ESAU AND JACOB - JOSEPH'S DREAMS

Jacob returns to Canaan

"Then the Lord said to Jacob, 'Go back to the land of your fathers and to your relatives, and I will be with you.'"- Genesis 31:3

During the years that Jacob spends in Harran with his uncle Laban, both Isaac and Rebecca die. The new head of the clan is now Jacob. But his brother Esau in the meantime has not forgotten the wrongs he has suffered. He just can't digest that famous dish of lentil soup.

Jacob, after obtaining Rachel as a wife returns to the land of Canaan where his father and his father's father are buried. But he learns that his brother Esau has organized a small army and is hunting him down there. Jacob plays cunning once again. Send explorers ahead to find out exactly where Esau is. The explorers return and report to Jacob,

"Behold, your brother comes to meet you with four hundred men." Jacob then addressed a prayer to his God, "God of my father Abraham and God of my father Isaac, you told me, 'Return to your homeland.' Save me now from the hands of my brother Esau because you promised me a large lineage like the sand of the sea."

After having addressed this prayer to God, Jacob sends a caravan of five servants to the brother, each with a herd of cattle, to give it to Esau. The servants were to tell Esau, *"Here is the gift your servant Jacob sends you."* He comes behind us. Jacob thought, *"I will appease him with these gifts and later I will introduce myself to him. Perhaps he will welcome me with kindness."- Genesis 32:20* While the servants go to meet Esau, Jacob spends a restless night in the camp.

Jacob struggles with God

"So Jacob was left alone, and a man wrestled with him till daybreak."- Genesis 32:24

During that night Jacob led the two wives and eleven children (Benjamin is not yet born) to go for the stream of Jabbok to get everyone safe. He remains alone. He trembles with fear. He fears his brother's revenge. Suddenly a man sneaks up and grabs him by the shoulders. Jacob in the dark does not understand who the unknown is.

In order not to be overwhelmed, he begins to fight fiercely with that shadow. The struggle lasts until the dawn comes. The unknown wrestler, unable to win Jacob, strikes him in the hip and Jacob's hip joint is dislocated. But Jacob still does not give up.

Then that strange apparition says, *"Leave me because the dawn has dawned." (Gen. 32:26)* And the voice is firm and sweet. Jacob understands that that man is the very personification of God. God wanted to convince Jacob that he has the strength to face his brother Esau. God fought with Jacob to give him courage. Then Jacob says to that shadow, *"I will not leave you unless you bless me first."* The Lord asks him, *"What's your name?"* Jacob answers.

Then the Lord says, "From this moment you will no longer be called Jacob, but Israel because you have fought with God and with men and you have won." (Gen. 32:28) Israel, in fact, means "he who is strong before God". From that night Jacob also takes the name of Israel. And Israel will also be called the chosen people descended from Jacob.

The meeting between Esau and Jacob

"Jacob looked up and there was Esau, coming with his four hundred men; so he divided the children among Leah, Rachel and the two female servants." - Genesis 33:1

Jacob, after fighting with God, finds strength and courage. His brother's fear has vanished along with the darkness of the night. Jacob feels completely transformed. The sun rises and Jacob sees Esau arrive escorted by the small army. Jacob goes to meet him and prostrates himself on the ground as a sign of friendship and reconciliation.

Esau already moved by the gifts and now by that signs of respect embraces his brother and kisses him. They both cry with emotion. Peace is now made. Then the two brothers separated and each settled in a different area of the land of Canaan.

Jacob moved to Shechem, near the valley of the Jordan River. There he buys a piece of land, he builds a house for himself and his family and some shelters for the flocks. The following spring the beloved wife Rachel dies giving birth to her last child. Jacob named him Benjamin which means "son of good omen".

Joseph's Dreams- Genesis 37

"Joseph had a dream, and when he told it to his brothers, they hated him all the more."-

Genesis 37:5

Jacob settles definitively in the land of Canaan. His twelve sons grow up healthy and robust and graze their father's flocks in the fertile valley of the Jordan. Even Joseph, the first son of Rachel, feeds the flock with his brothers. At home, with old Jacob, there remains only Benjamin who is still a child. Jacob, of all the sons, prefers the last two because they were given to him by the beloved bride. To his son Joseph, Jacob gives a tunic with long sleeves. And the older brothers are jealous of him. Joseph is now 17 years old.

One night he had a dream and the next morning he told his brothers, "We were tying the sheaves in the middle of the countryside, when my sheaf stood up and stood upright and your sheaves came around and prostrated themselves before mine."(37:6) Another night Joseph still has a dream and tells his father and brothers, "The sun, the moon and eleven stars prostrated themselves before me." (37:9) Jacob rebukes him and tells him, "What a dream this is! Should your mother and I and your brothers come to bow down before you?" And the brothers say full of anger, "Do you want to reign over us and want to dominate us?"

And since then his brothers have begun to hate him more and more and wait for a favourable opportunity to take revenge on him.

PART 5
JOSEPH SOLD BY HIS BROTHERS - JOSEPH IN PRISON - PHARAOH'S DREAMS - JOSEPH MET HIS BROTHERS

Joseph sold by the brothers

"So when the Midianite merchants came by, his brothers pulled Joseph up out of the cistern and sold him for twenty shekels of silver to the Ishmaelites, who took him to Egypt."- Gen. 37:28

The opportunity presents itself as soon as possible. One day Joseph's brothers are grazing. Joseph stayed at home this time. Jacob says to his son, *"Joseph, go to your brothers to see how they are, then come back to tell me." (37:12)* Joseph, obedient, does as his father commanded him. When the brothers, camped by a shallow and dry well, see it from afar they say to each other,

"Here comes the dreamer! Let's kill him and throw him in this well. Then we will tell our father that a ferocious beast has devoured him. So we'll see what happens to his dreams!" (37:19-20)

But Reuben, the eldest, opposes, *"My brothers, we do not shed his blood. Let's throw him alive in the well. He will die of thirst."* He intended, however, to save him secretly and bring him back to his father.

When Joseph arrives, the brothers, following Ruben's advice, tear off his long-sleeved tunic and throw him alive into the well. Then they sit down to eat. Now they look up and see a caravan of merchants coming to Egypt. Judas, one of the brothers, suggests to the others, *"What's the gain in killing Joseph? If we leave him in the well he will surely die of thirst. Rather, let's sell him to those merchants."*

The proposal is liked and Joseph is extracted from the well and is sold as a slave for twenty silver coins to the merchants. The brothers then take the long-sleeved tunic, dirty it with the blood of a kid and send it to Jacob with these words, *"We found it. Find out if it's your son's tunic."* Jacob recognizes her easily and exclaims full of anguish, *"It is my son's tunic! A fierce beast has devoured him!"* For many days old Jacob cries the death of his son. And nobody can comfort him.

Joseph in prison- Genesis 39

"Joseph's master took him and put him in prison, the place where the king's prisoners were confined. But while Joseph was there in the prison, the Lord was with him; he showed him kindness and granted him

favor in the eyes of the prison warden."- Gen. 39:20-21

The merchants arrive in Egypt and sell Joseph to Potiphar, an adviser to the pharaoh and commander of the palace guards. Potiphar has a very beautiful wife, but also unfaithful. The woman immediately falls in love with the young Jewish slave and tries to seduce him. But Joseph rejects the proposal of scandal. Then the woman, points in pride, grabs Joseph for the dress and tries to embrace him with force. Joseph struggles. The dress tears and remains in the woman's hands and Joseph run away. (39:12)The woman begins to scream with how much breath she has in her throat,

"So, come see servants! See, the Jew tried to rape me. I screamed and he, leaving the robe beside me, fled."

When Potiphar hears his wife's story, he gets angry. He seeks Joseph and has him imprisoned. The cupbearer and the baker of the pharaoh are also locked up in Joseph's cell.

One night, the two make each a dream. In the morning they tell their cellmate, Joseph. The butler says, "I was in front of a vine plant from which clusters of ripe grapes hung. I took the grapes, squeezed them in Pharaoh's cup and offered it to him to drink." Joseph replies, "The dream means that you will soon be free and will still serve the pharaoh."

(40:9-13) Even the baker tells Joseph his dream because he interprets it, "I kept bread baskets on the head. But while I was taking them to the pharaoh, some birds pecked at the bread in the baskets." Joseph answers, "I'm sorry, friend, but yours is a bad dream. The Pharaoh will soon have you hanged and the birds will come to catch your body." (40:) In reality it happens as Joseph had predicted.

Pharaoh's dreams

"When two full years had passed, Pharaoh had a dream: He was standing by the Nile, when out of the river there came up seven cows, sleek and fat, and they grazed among the reeds. After them, seven other cows, ugly and gaunt, came up out of the Nile and stood beside those on the riverbank. And the cows that were ugly and gaunt ate up the seven sleek, fat cows. Then Pharaoh woke up."- Gen. 41:1-4

Pharaoh also makes a strange dream one night. He feels like he's at the Nile. And here seven beautiful and fat cows come up from the river to graze among the rushes of the shore. After that, seven other cows ascend from the Nile. But the latter is ugly and thin. They too stop next to the first on the bank of the Nile. At a certain point, the lean cows assault the fat ones and in a few moments, they devour them. At that moment the pharaoh wakes up all sweaty and agitated.

Slowly she calms down, turns in bed and goes back to sleep. And here is a second dream very similar to the previous one. Seven big and beautiful ears sprout from a single stem. After that, another seven ears sprout up and burned by the wind. And immediately the empty ears swallow the big and beautiful ones. Again the Pharaoh wakes up, more and more agitated and perplexed.

At that time a lot of importance was attached to dreams and people often adjusted themselves to them. "What do these dreams mean?" asks the Pharaoh of Egypt. As soon as the day comes, he calls all his soothsayers to the palace. But nobody knows how to give a convincing explanation. Then the chief cupbearer who had been in prison with Joseph says

, "There is a young Jew in prison who has interpreted a dream of mine. And just as he had predicted, it happened."

Then, Pharaoh summons Joseph and sends his soothsayers. The guards immediately take Joseph out of prison. He shaves his head as was the custom with the Egyptians; he changes his clothes and presents himself before the pharaoh. After listening to the story of dreams, Joseph explains,

"The seven fat cows and the seven full ears want to mean this: they are about to come seven years of great abundance in the whole country of Egypt. The seven lean cows and the seven empty ears

mean this: there will be seven years of famine after abundance."

Now Pharaoh arranges things in such a way that, during abundance, the grain is stored in warehouses in cities. These provisions will serve for years of famine. Thus the inhabitants of the country will not be decimated by hunger. Pharaoh and his ministers like the interpretation of dreams and Joseph's advice. Indeed the pharaoh, struck by the wisdom of Joseph, puts him at the head of the whole operation of gathering and distributing food during the years of abundance and famine.

Joseph meets the brothers

"Now Joseph was the governor of the land, the person who sold grain to its entire people. So when Joseph's brothers arrived, they bowed down to him with their faces to the ground. As soon as Joseph saw his brothers, he recognized them, but he pretended to be a stranger and spoke harshly to them. 'Where do you come from?' he asked. 'From the land of Canaan,' they replied, 'to buy food.'" - Gen. 42:6-7

During the years of abundance, Joseph had the grain stored in the city stores. When the years of famine begin and the people begin to feel the pangs of hunger, the Pharaoh tells the Egyptians, "Go to Joseph and do what he tells you." Then Joseph opens the stores and sells the grain to the Egyptians. Caravans also come from other countries in Egypt to buy grain because famine has hit the entire Middle East area, from the Nile to the Euphrates River. Old Jacob who lives with his children in the land of Canaan learns that there is plenty of grain in Egypt.

So one day he tells his children, "Go down there and buy corn for us because we can keep ourselves alive and not die." The te3n brothers of Joseph, excluding Benjamin the smallest set off with a caravan of donkeys towards the land of Egypt. They arrive before Joseph who immediately recognizes them. They, on the other hand, do not even remotely imagine having their brother in front of them who they had sold as a slave. Joseph feigns the utmost indifference. Indeed, using a harsh and contemptuous tone, he asks the prostrate brothers with their faces on the ground, "Where do you come from?" "We come from the land of Canaan," they answer, "to buy food." "You are spies!" accuses them, Joseph. "You have come to see the uncovered points of my country." "No, sir," the frightened brothers justify themselves, "we have come for food." "We are brothers, children of one man. We are...we were twelve. But the youngest is now with our father and one...one is gone." "I want to test you." Joseph replies always with an authoritative tone "Send one of you to take your younger brother. The others will remain my prisoners. If you really have another brother, I will believe you. If not, for the life of the pharaoh, you are spies!"

For three days Joseph keeps his brothers in prison. Then, filled with compassion, he tells them, "Go to Canaan and bring your younger brother here. But one of you will stay here." And, having chosen Simeon among them, he has them chained before their eyes. Prostrated with their faces on the ground, Joseph's brothers are terrified. The dream of sheaves that Joseph had made so many years before has now come true.

PART 6
THE RETURN OF THE BROTHERS WITH BENJAMIN - JOSEPH MAKES HIMSELF KNOWN - JACOB'S CLAN MOVES TO EGYPT

The return of the brothers with Benjamin

"So the men took the gifts and double the amount of silver, and Benjamin also. They hurried down to Egypt and presented themselves to Joseph."- Gen. 43:15

Before the nine brothers left for Canaan, Joseph ordered the guards to fill their sacks with wheat and to return the money they had each paid for the purchase in the respective bag. The sons of Jacob load the sacks on the donkeys and leave. After a day of walking, they stop at a place to spend the night. One of the brothers opens his sack to feed the donkey and sees the money at the mouth of the sack. The others also open the bags and everyone finds their own money. Then frightened they ask themselves, *"What does this mean?"* When they come from Jacob they report all the events agitated. The old man, hearing the story of his children, says crying, *"You have deprived me of children!"* Joseph is gone. Simeon is a prisoner and Benjamin, my little Benjamin, you want to take me. Then Ruben, the elder, says, *"Father, give me Benjamin. I promise you that I will return it to you."*

Finally, Jacob agrees and lets Benjamin leave. For the second time, the ten brothers set off with their donkeys towards the land of Egypt. When Joseph sees Benjamin with them, a knot of tears rises in his throat. But he still feigns the utmost indifference,

"This would be the younger brother you told me about?" Joseph questions. "Yes, my lord - the prostrate brothers answer with their faces to the ground."

Joseph makes the brothers serve an abundant meal. Then he had their sacks filled with grain and, in Benjamin's, he had his servants hide a precious silver cup.

In the morning the ten brothers leave. They have just left the city; when Joseph tells the chief of the guards, *"Soon, follow those men. Accuse them of theft and bring them back here."* The head of the guards joins the brothers and accuses them of theft. Then they, declaring themselves innocent, hurry to open their bags. And the cup is found in Benjamin's sack. They were brought back before Joseph; they weep and fall to the ground. Joseph tells them, *"What action have you committed?"* Benjamin will remain my prisoner. Then Judas raises his head from the ground and says to Joseph with a trembling voice, *"My lord, we cannot return to our father without Benjamin."* He has already suffered the pain of another child torn by a ferocious beast and another pain so great will kill him.

Joseph makes himself known

"Then Joseph could no longer control himself before all his attendants, and he cried out, 'Have everyone leave my presence!' So there was no one with Joseph when he made himself known to his brothers. And he wept so loudly that the Egyptians heard him, and Pharaoh's household heard about it." - Gen. 45: 1-2

At those words, Joseph can no longer hold back his tears. Forget all the wrongs suffered by the brothers, forget the well where they had thrown him, forget the time spent in slavery and in prison. Joseph casts his arms around the brothers' necks and with a broken voice says, *"I am Joseph. Does my father still live?"* The brothers do not believe their eyes. They are still not convinced that they are in the presence of their brother. They are dismayed and fear another trap. But Joseph continues: *"I am your brother, who you sold for twenty silver coins."* Tell my father the glory I have in Egypt and bring it here. Then he squeezes Benjamin to his chest and covers him with kisses. Then finally the brothers are convinced and, bursting into tears, embrace Joseph. They ask for forgiveness, they laugh, they cry, they talk about old Jacob and

Joseph who welcomes and forgives the brothers, despite the evil that they did to him, resembles Jesus.

Even Jesus will be sold, he will be treated by men like a slave, and he will be put in prison and will be crucified. But from the cross, Jesus will forgive his crucifiers and all men. God, in his project of salvation, wanting to prepare the coming of Jesus, presents to humanity the figure of Joseph so that we can understand right now how the true saviour will behave.

Jacob's clan moves to Egypt

"So Joseph settled his father and his brothers in Egypt and gave them property in the best part of the land, the district of Rameses, as Pharaoh directed. Joseph also provided his father and his brothers and his entire father's household with food, according to the number of their children."- Gen. 47:11-12

After being recognized, Joseph sends the eleven brothers to Canaan with abundant provisions and gifts. As soon as they see Jacob they say they are very excited: - Father, Joseph is alive, indeed the rules Egypt! But the heart of old Jacob remains cold. He cannot believe, he does not want to believe in the words of his children. Only after seeing the donkeys loaded with wheat and the gifts, Jacob is convinced. At the height of joy he exclaims, *"Enough! Joseph, my son, is alive. I'll go see it before I die."* That same night Jacob still hears the firm and sweetest voice of his God, "Jacob, Jacob!, says the voice. "Here I am," the old man replies with the same readiness as Isaac his father and Abraham, his father's father. The voice resumes,

"I am the God of your father and of your father's father. Do not be afraid to go to Egypt because there I will make you a great people."

Joseph learns that his father is going with a caravan towards Egypt.

Then he has his chariot attacked and runs towards him. As soon as he sees it he throws his arms around his neck and cries for a long time with his head on the old man's shoulder. Jacob caresses his son's head and says, *"Now I can also die because I saw your face."*

In the story of Joseph, there are no direct interventions by God. God does not speak to Joseph as he spoke to his fathers. It seems that in this story everything takes place according to human logic. But God also indirectly uses human facts to carry out his project of salvation. Because of Joseph, Jacob's clan settled permanently in Egypt, leaving the land of Canaan. In Egypt, the Jews are welcomed with all the honours and the pharaoh grants them vast lands east of the Nile for pastures. In Egypt, Jacob, Joseph and his brothers die. But the descendants of Jacob and his sons multiply.

The people of Israel become *"as numerous as the stars"*. But in this way God has only fulfilled one of the promises though Israel is still in a foreign land. When will God grant the land of Canaan, the Promised Land, to his people in perpetual possession? The years pass. The pharaohs succeed each other on the throne of Egypt. The Jews who had been welcomed east of the Nile, in the land of Goshen, as guests of honour, are now treated like slaves. A new era is opening up for the chosen people and for humanity. The story of the patriarchs Abraham, Isaac and Jacob ends. The story of the greatest character of the Old Testament begins Moses, the prophet, the condottiere, the liberator, the legislator. Moses, the one who spoke face to face with God. With the story of Joseph's death, the first book of the Bible called Genesis ends. The story of Moses is narrated in the following four books: Exodus, Leviticus, Numbers and Deuteronomy. These books, together with Genesis, form a single block called Pentateuch (= five books).

THE HISTORY OF MOSES
(Exodus - Leviticus - Numbers - Deuteronomy)

PART 1
OPPRESSION OF THE PEOPLE OF ISRAEL - MOSES SAVED FROM THE NILE - THE FLIGHT OF MOSES - THE BURNING BUSH

Oppression of the people of Israel

"So they put slave masters over them to oppress them with forced labor, and they built Pithom and Rameses as store cities for Pharaoh. But the more they were oppressed, the more they multiplied and spread; so the Egyptians came to dread the Israelites and worked them ruthlessly. They made their lives bitter with harsh labor in brick and mortar and with all kinds of work in the fields; in all their harsh labor the Egyptians worked them ruthlessly."- Ex. 1:11-14

The people of Israel have been in Egypt for 400 years now. During this long period of time, there have been numerous pharaoh dynasties. New monuments rise next to the ancient pyramids built a thousand years before Abraham. We are about 1250 BC. The pharaoh Ramses II now sits on the throne of Egypt. By now Joseph's story has been forgotten. The new Pharaoh is worried about the growth of Israel which occupies the land of Goshen east of the Nile. Jews are a people within a people.

One day the new pharaoh tells his subjects, "Behold, the people of the children of Israel are larger and stronger than us. We take measures to prevent it from increasing its power. Otherwise, in case of war, Israel will join our enemies and occupy our country." From that day on, Jews no longer had the freedom to move with their flocks, nor to cultivate the land that had been given to them. Instead, they are forced to work as builders, a job they had never practised. They knead the clay to make bricks that they then cook in the sun. They must build defence walls and irrigation canals under the lash of Egyptian overseers. For people accustomed to the freedom of large spaces, to mobility, this condition is unbearable. To this first restriction is added soon a more serious decision of the pharaoh. The Jewish midwives are ordered to kill all the males of Israel at the time of birth.

Moses saved from the Nile

"Then Pharaoh's daughter went down to the Nile to bathe, and her attendants were walking along the riverbank. She saw the basket among the reeds and sent her female slave to get it. She opened it and saw the baby. He was crying, and she felt sorry for him. 'This is one of the Hebrew babies,' she said." - Ex. 2:5-6

A Jewish family that already had two children, Miriam and Aaron, is cheered up by a third child. The mother, who had given birth without the help of the midwife, thinks of hiding it to save his life. The thing succeeds for about three months. But every now and then the Jewish houses are searched by the Egyptian guards. That mother then locks the child in a waterproof wicker basket which she then entrusts to the waters of the Nile. The child's sister, Miriam, hides among the rushes on the riverbank to observe from afar what happens to her little brother. And here is the pharaoh's daughter going down to the Nile to bathe, while her maids walked along the shore. The basket got caught in the rushes. Pharaoh's daughter sends a slave to collect it. He opens it and sees a beautiful baby crying with small fists on his eyes.

Pharaoh's daughter feels great tenderness and says, *"He must be a Jewish child."* Miriam then comes out of hiding and suggests to the princess, *"If you want, I can find a Jewish woman who nurses the baby for you."* *"All right,"* the pharaoh's daughter replies that she immediately became fond of that little boy. Mary naturally calls her mother, who can thus get her little son back. When the child grew up and became a youth, the mother leads him to the pharaoh's daughter. And the boy becomes like a son to her and she calls him Moses which means *"saved from the waters"*.

The flight of Moses

"When Pharaoh heard of this, he tried to kill Moses, but Moses fled from Pharaoh and went to live in Midian, where he sat down by a well." - Ex. 2:15

Moses is raised in the court of the Pharaoh in the midst of comforts and riches. However, he knows he is Jewish and does not forget his people. One day he goes to the land of Goshen where Israel resides and notes the heavy jobs that the people are forced to perform.

Moses sees an Egyptian overseer striking a Jewish worker. Immediately it turns on with indignation. He looks around. He sees no other supervisors. Moses then strikes the Egyptian to death and buries him in the sand. The next day Moses observes two Jews who are bickering. He intervenes to divide them and one of them tells him,

"With what right do you want to be a judge between us? Do you want to kill me like you killed the Egyptian yesterday?"

Moses then realizes that the fact of the previous day is already in the public domain. The pharaoh himself has been warned and now he is looking for Moses to put him to death. Moses, seized by fear, leaves Egypt and takes refuge in the country of Midian, east of the Sinai Peninsula, beyond the Gulf of Aqaba.

In that territory live also some Jewish descendants of the patriarch Abraham. These Jews had not gone to

Egypt at the time of Joseph, son of Jacob, but they had remained free shepherds in the desert. Unlike the Jews who were in Egypt, the Midianites had retained a certain memory of the God of Abraham, Isaac and Jacob. Moses, therefore, wanders like a fugitive through the lands of Midian.

One day, distraught and dejected, he sits at a well. In the neighbourhood lives a man named Jethro who has seven daughters. And behold, these young women come to the well where Moses sits to draw water and make their father's flock drink. Just at that moment some peasant shepherds arrive and chase away Jethro's daughters. Moses, faced with this abuse, rediscovers his strength. He gets up in all his imposing stature and, by dint of pushing, drives those bullies away. The girls, back home, talk about Moses' intervention to their father and him, to reward the defender of the daughters, hosts him at home and gives him his daughter Zipporah as a wife.

The burning bush

"Now Moses was tending the flock of Jethro his father-in-law, the priest of Midian, and he led the flock to the far side of the wilderness and came to Horeb, the mountain of God. There the angel of the Lord appeared to him in flames of fire from within a bush. Moses saw that though the bush was on fire it did not burn up."- Ex. 3:1-2

Some years pass. Moses is now part of the Jethro
and grazes his father-in-law's flocks. Pharao
Ramses II in the meantime dies and he is succeeded
by Mernepta. The new Pharaoh is even more cruel
and decisive than the previous one and continues to
oppress the people of Israel. One day Moses, who is
now about forty years old, leads the flock of Jethro to
the slopes of Mount Sinai, south of the peninsula of
the same name. And here Moses sees tongues of fire
coming out of a bush.

At a safe distance, Moses observes that fire waiting
for it to go out after consuming the brambles. But the
fire continues and the bush is not consumed. Then
Moses thinks, *"I want to get closer because this is a
truly exceptional show. Why does the bush not
burn?"* Moses is about to approach the burning bush
when he hears a voice. It is the same voice, firm and
sweet that had spoken to Abraham, Isaac and Jacob.
"Moses, Moses!" says the voice. And Moses, like
Abraham, like Isaac and like Jacob, promptly replies,
"Here I am!" The voice resumes,

*"Don't get close. Take off your sandals because
the place where you are is holy. I am the God of
Abraham, the God of Isaac and the God of Jacob.
I observed the condition of my people in Egypt and
I decided to free him and give him the land I
promised to Abraham, Isaac and Jacob. Therefore,
get Israel out of Egypt. I will be with you."*

PART 2

REVEALS HIS NAME -
RETURNS TO EGYPT -
FIRST NINE PLAGUES -
THE PASSAGE OF THE
EXTERMINATOR

God reveals his name

"'This is my name forever, the name you shall call me from generation to generation.'"- Ex. 3:15

Moses stops scared. He looks towards the bush that continues to burn without being consumed and says, almost speaking to himself,

"Who am I to go to the Pharaoh and to get the Israelites out of Egypt? They will tell me. Who sent you? And what will I answer them?"

And the voice, firm and sweet, says, *"I am God."* God in Hebrew is the third person of the verb to be both in the present time and in the future time. God, therefore, can be translated in two ways: He is or He will be. Revealing this name God defines himself as He who is or He who will always be with you (Moses). Or, better yet, the name could be translated with a whole sentence: You will know who I am from the works I will do for Israel. Or: I am the One who will free Israel. I am the One who will save humanity. Thus, in the name that God reveals to Moses, his whole plan of salvation is enclosed. It is as if God said: From the facts that I will accomplish you will also understand my nature. The name, among the Jews, always indicates also the mission of those who wear it. The whole person is in the name. Revealing his name to Moses, God relies on him and entrusts himself to all humanity. God shows that he trusts men, that he loves them. From this moment God has a proper name. He will no longer be called El, which means God generically, but God: He who is. Moses, after receiving the assurance of his help from God, again objects,

"But I am not a good talker. How can I convince Pharaoh to liberate Israel?" And God replies, "Who gave the man a mouth? Am I not Jehovah? Your brother Aaron will help you in the mission and he will speak for you."

Moses returns to Egypt

"Then Moses went back to Jethro his father-in-law and said to him, 'Let me return to my own people in Egypt to see if any of them are still alive.'" - Ex. 4:18

After 400 years God has not forgotten the promises made to Abraham, Isaac and Jacob. The slavery of Egypt served Israel to understand how without God man cannot be realized. Without God, we become slaves of other men. Without God there is no future, there is no freedom, there is no equality for men. The strong oppress the weak, violence reigns. This is the sad condition from which God wants to free not only Israel but all humanity. The mission of Moses thus anticipates the far more important and definitive mission of Jesus. Moses will free Israel from the slavery of Pharaoh; Jesus will free men from the slavery of sin, selfishness, violence, hatred, death. Moses, therefore, takes courage and returns to Egypt to carry out the mission that God has entrusted to him. Before entering Egypt, Moses meets the brother Aaron of a few years older than him. Together they present themselves to the pharaoh and ask for freedom for Israel. After listening to the request of the two brothers, the guffaw pharaoh replies: - Who is this Jahveh why should I listen to his voice? I do not know any God. I have my gods: Amon and King, the personification of the rising and setting sun, and then Osiris and Isis his wife and sister and their son Horus, of whom I, the Pharaoh Mernepta, am the reincarnation. Am I the servant of God who must follow his orders? From that day the Pharaoh becomes, even more, demanding with the Jews; it aggravates them with new jobs and makes surveillance even more rigid.

The first nine plagues

"Then the Lord said to Moses, 'See, I have made you like God to Pharaoh, and your brother Aaron will be your prophet. You are to say everything I command you, and your brother Aaron is to tell Pharaoh to let the Israelites go out of his country. But I will harden

90

Pharaoh's heart, and though I multiply my signs and wonders in Egypt, he will not listen to you. Then I will lay my hand on Egypt and with mighty acts of judgment I will bring out my divisions, my people the Israelites. And the Egyptians will know that I am the Lord when I stretch out my hand against Egypt and bring the Israelites out of it.'" – Ex. 7:1-5

Moses, to carry out the mission that God has entrusted to him, must fight on two fronts. On the one hand, he must convince his people and lead them to faith in God; on the other hand, it must fight against the power of the pharaoh who does not intend to renounce the cheap Jewish labour. But God, as he had promised by the burning bush, is on the side of Moses and Aaron. To convince Israel and the pharaoh of its power, God uses some natural calamities that normally fell in Egypt, intensifying them and using them as instruments of persuasion.

Often the waters of the Nile become muddy and red due to an alga that grows there sometimes in a huge way. At other times it is the frogs that multiply beyond the norm and destroy the crops. Or they are mosquitoes and flies invading houses and stables. Even the plague or the winds that break down and dry are completely natural events. But while Moses insists with the pharaoh to leave Israel free, those calamities become more serious and insistent. After each of these natural disasters, which the Bible calls "plagues", the pharaoh always seems about to yield to the request of Moses, but later, in retrospect, retracted and stubborn. His heart gets harder and harder. He doesn't want to give up. He doesn't want to give up. He does not want to admit that God, the god of those Jewish slaves, of those beggars, is more powerful than his gods Amon and King, the personification of the rising and setting sun, Osiris and Isis, his wife and sister, and Horus of whom he considers reincarnation.

"A god like me - thinks Pharaoh - cannot yield to the pressures of another god, a god of slaves and beggars."

Thus thinks the proud pharaoh of the land of Egypt, Mernepta, lord of the High and Low Nile.

The passage of the exterminator

"'On that same night I will pass through Egypt and strike down every firstborn of both people and animals, and I will bring judgment on all the gods of Egypt. I am the Lord. The blood will be a sign for you on the houses where you are, and when I see the blood, I will pass over you. No destructive plague will touch you when I strike Egypt.'"- Ex. 12:12-13

The people of Israel, before being enslaved in Egypt and since the time of Abraham, had kept a rite linked to pastoral activity. At the beginning of each spring, the shepherds began to move with the flocks to go to the steppe where the rains had made the grass grow.

To remove the diseases that were attributed to an evil power from the flock, before leaving for the pastures, the shepherds sacrificed a lamb and sprinkled the pegs of the tents with his blood. The evil power, or the devastator or exterminator as it was called, carrying disease and death, seeing the bloodshed on the pegs, would have had to pass over without causing damage. The innocent blood of the lamb was considered a protective amulet. The sacrificed lamb was then eaten standing up shortly before leaving for the pastures when the shepherds were already dressed for the journey. Lamb was eaten as a side dish of bitter herbs that grew in the desert.

This ancient rite was called Easter or passage. And it is precisely this rite that God suggests to Moses that he should resume before leaving Egypt. Like the ancient shepherds of Abraham's time, the Israelites would have had to sacrifice a lamb and with its blood mark the doors of the houses where they lived. During the night, the exterminator, this time representative of the power of God, would have passed through Egypt killing all the firstborn of Egyptian families and saving the Jewish houses. It is the last "plague" that Moses threatens to the pharaoh. But this time to Mernepta is not too scared. He does not believe in the power of God, the god of slaves and beggars. He hopes for the protection of Amon and King, of Osiris and Isis, of their son Horus. "A god like me - thinks the pharaoh - is not afraid of the threats of a foreign god, who perhaps does not even exist". Thus the proud Mernepta, lord of the land of Egypt, of the Nile Valley and of the Delta thinks wrongly.

PART 3

THE EXIT FROM EGYPT - II PASSAGE OF THE RED SEA - IN THE DESERT TOWARDS SINAI - THE SINAI ALLIANCE

The exit from Egypt

"During the night Pharaoh summoned Moses and Aaron and said, 'Up! Leave my people, you and the Israelites! Go, worship the Lord as you have requested.'"- Ex. 12:31

The Israelites faithfully carry out the indications of Moses. During the night every firstborn of Egyptian families die. The pharaoh is convinced this time that the God of Moses and Aaron are far more powerful than his gods. In the heart of that same night he hastily summons Moses and Aaron to the palace and, in a gentle and obsequious tone, tells them, "Go ahead, you and your people, and go to serve your God. Take your cattle too and your flocks and games! And bless me too!"

At daybreak, all the people of Israel, estimated at around 60,000, finally leave Egypt heading towards Canaan, the Promised Land. To go to Canaan the Israelites could choose three caravans. The most used was the road to the north or via dei Filistei which, bordering the Mediterranean arrived in Gaza on the coast of Palestine as it was also called the land of Canaan. The second road called Delle Carovane, it passed through the centre of the Sinai Peninsula and reached the port of Elat on the northern tip of the Gulf of Aqaba. The third, finally, was the western road that descended along the east coast of the Red Sea, reached the Sinai massif and then ascended as far as the Kades oasis on the southern borders of the land of Canaan.

Moses chooses this last itinerary, not only because it is considered safer, but above all, because he intends to revisit Mount Sinai where God had entrusted him with the mission to free Israel as if to prove to God that the mission had been accomplished. But to take the western road it was first necessary to cross the Red Sea. The water, where Moses decides to pass, is low. More than anything else it is about crossing the brackish water marshes subject to the tide. Those marshes are called Bitter Lakes.

The passage of the Red Sea

"When Pharaoh let the people go, God did not lead them on the road through the Philistine country, though that was shorter. For God said, 'If they face war, they might change their minds and return to Egypt.' So God led the people around by the desert road toward the Red Sea. The Israelites went up out of Egypt ready for battle." - Ex. 13:17-18

When Israel is now near the western shore of the Bitter Lakes, the pharaoh once again regrets having succumbed to Moses' request. *"I hurt these slaves to leave!"* says the pharaoh to his ministers. *"So they can no longer serve us."* Then he makes the horses attach to his chariot of war and takes with him the flower of the army: six hundred chariots with as many knights armed with bows and spears. The Egyptian army, raising a cloud of dust, chases and reaches the Jews.

When the Israelites see that cloud of dust approaching, they turn to Moses and tell him with a certain sarcasm mixed with dismay,

"Perhaps there were no tombs in Egypt that you brought us to die in the desert?" Moses replies "Do not be afraid. Be strong because God is with us. The Egyptians you see will never see them again. God will fight for you. He is the God of hosts."

Then Moses rises in all his imposing stature and extends his right arm over the salt marshes. A strong east wind blows throughout the night and, in conjunction with low tide, pushes the waters of the Bitter Lakes. A muddy but practicable tongue of land appears. Israel thus crosses the Red Sea "on dry feet". The Egyptian army that pursues the fugitives closely rushes into the gap that the wind and low tide have created across the sea. But the heavy war chariots of the Pharaoh's army sink into the soft sand and mud.

Then suddenly the east wind stops blowing and the tide starts to rise again. The waters of the Red Sea rise and submerge, between the shouts of victory of the Israelites and those of panic of the Egyptians, the flower of the Pharaoh's army. The passage of the Red Sea has always been interpreted by Israel as the most extraordinary intervention of God in favour of his people. For Israel, the Red Sea is not simply a geographical boundary between the land of slavery and the desert, the land of freedom. The waters that save the Jews and submerge the Egyptians are the very image of God who saves those who trust in him while abandoning those who reject him to their own destiny. The passage of the Red Sea will remain for Israel the most important and prodigious proof of the power of God, Lord of armies. Arriving on the eastern shore of the sea, Israel expresses its own feelings of gratitude to Jehovah with a song sung by Miriam, sister of Moses and Aaron: I want to sing in honour of God: because he has marvelously triumphed, he has thrown horse and rider into the sea. God is brave in war, his name is God. Pharaoh's chariots and his army threw into the sea and his chosen fighters were submerged in the Red Sea. The depths covered them, they sank like stone.

In the desert towards Sinai

"The whole Israelite community set out from Elim and came to the Desert of Sin, which is between Elim and Sinai, on the fifteenth day of the second month

after they had come out of Egypt. In the desert the whole community grumbled against Moses and Aaron. The Israelites said to them, 'If only we had died by the Lord's hand in Egypt! There we sat around pots of meat and ate all the food we wanted, but you have brought us out into this desert to starve this entire assembly to death.'"- Exodus 16:1-3

After crossing the Red Sea on dry land, Israel is finally free in the desert. But the desert does not only represent the regained freedom. A desert is also a place of deprivation and conflict. Israel will remain in the desert for forty years, a symbolic number indicating the passage of an entire generation. Not the men who came out of Egypt will enter the Promised Land, but their children. Not even Moses will tread on the land of Canaan. He will see the homeland dreamed from afar, he will possess it only with his eyes. This long pilgrimage of Israel in the desert is like a test to which God subjects his people to convince them that only in the abandonment in him can they be realized. In the desert, Israel experiences that the survival of every day is a gift from God.

In the desert, regrets for the past and programs for the future are not allowed. In the desert, you have to live for the day entrusting yourself completely to God. The same teaching that one day will be proposed by Jesus. Man must not regret the past, nor fear the future. He has pain every day. Man must first seek the things of God and then those that concern the

99

body. Thus Jesus will teach. In the desert, Israel experiences these truths. In the desert, Israel purifies its faith. In the desert he will meet God, he will become a people, and he will become aware of his own strength supported by the power of God.

At the Red Sea God divides the waters from the dry earth. It is the same action that God performed at the dawn of creation. The desert is starting all over again. The desert is a new land; it is like the earth on the first day of creation. In the desert especially Israel is called to pre-empt the needs of the spirit to those of the body. However, Israel will not always pass the desert test. In the desert, Israel regrets the meat it ate in Egypt. He regrets the onions of Egypt now that he has only sand. But God, once again, is patient with those he loves. He tells Moses, *"I heard the murmuring of the Israelites."* **Talk to them like this,** *"At sunset, you will eat meat and in the morning you will be filled with bread."* Israel will, in fact, feed on quails and manna. God still uses natural events to manifest his power and providence.

The quail migrating cross the Sinai Peninsula and often fall to the ground exhausted. Manna is an edible resin produced by the tamarisk plant that grows in the desert. Israel does not even pass the test of thirst. He complains to Moses, *"Why did you make us come out of Egypt to make us, our children and our cattle die of thirst?"* And God brings water out of the rock and quenches his people. Quail, manna and water that flow from the rock is the symbol of the power of God, but also of his patience. God tests Israel and then satisfies its needs. Moses himself does not completely pass the desert test. He too, at the locality of Meriba, doubts for an instant the word of God and strikes the rock twice with a stick to bring forth the water. For this, he will see only the land of Canaan without being able to enter.

The Sinai alliance

The desert is above all the place where Israel meets its God in a solemn and official manner. In the desert, Israel, which before was a non-people, a bunch of slaves without a future, without legislation, without an organization, becomes a people. The meeting between Israel and God takes place on the sacred mountain, on that mountain where God had already spoken to his servant Moses. Israel descends along the Sinai Peninsula and reaches the slopes of the mountain massif that gives its name to the whole peninsula. It almost seems that God has attracted him to that place for an important appointment, for a love appointment.

On the slopes, between the gorges and the peaks of that mountain massif, God reveals himself majestically to Moses and to all the people. The manifestation of God on Mount Sinai is the most spectacular of all those described in the Bible. God is revealed through terrifying natural phenomena. A dense cloud covers the mountain. Then there is a violent storm. Lightning and thunder shake them as if there was an earthquake and a volcanic eruption and then smoke and fire and howl of the wind among the gorges of the mountain.

While terrified Israel is at the foot of the mountain, Moses rises alone on the peaks to meet his terrible and sweet God face to face. On Mount God reveals to his servant the terms of a new alliance. The Sinai covenant is a deepening of the covenants already made by God with Noah and Abraham. This time the covenant is between God and all the people. Moses is only the mediator, the intermediary of this pact. The Sinai alliance follows the treaties of subjection which, at that time, the kings established with their own vassals.

According to these treaties, the king, after having introduced himself and having listed his own merits, established the norms that the vassals had to observe. For his part, the king offered protection and aid to those who had observed his pacts. According to this scheme, the alliance between God and Israel also takes place. God presents himself to Moses as the only God. Like the God who brought Israel out of the condition of slavery. Then, God sets the norms that the people must observe. These are the ten commands, or the ten words, which summarize the duties of Israel towards God and towards others.

PART 4
THE TEN COMMANDMENTS - ISRAEL'S FIRST TRANSGRESSION - TRAVELING TO CANAAN - THE DEATH OF MOSES

Ten Commandments

"So Moses went back and summoned the elders of the people and set before them all the words the Lord had commanded him to speak."- Exodus 19:7

God pronounces on Sinai words that remain carved in the mind of Moses. The Bible, with a symbolic language, reports that God himself sculpts these words on the stone. But it is probably Moses who, during his stay on the Sinai, transfers the words of God to two large slabs of stone. These are *"the ten words" of God. (Ex. 20:1-17):*

- I am God, your God, who brought you out of the land of Egypt, from the condition of slavery. You will have no other gods in front of me. You will not bow down to them and you will not serve them because I, God, am your God, a jealous God.

- You will not pronounce in vain the name of God, your God.
- Remember the Sabbath day to sanctify it. Six days you will struggle and you will do your job. But the seventh day is the Sabbath in honour of God.
- Honour your father and your mother.
- Do not kill.
- Do not commit adultery.
- Do not steal.
- Do not bear false witness against your neighbour.
- Do not wish for your neighbour's house.
- Do not covet your neighbour's wife.

While God speaks to his servant in the dark cloud, the people perceive the thunder and lightning and the wind between the throats like the sound of a horn and sees the Sinai smoking like a volcano.

Israel's first transgression

"When the people saw that Moses was so long in coming down from the mountain, they gathered around Aaron and said, 'Come, make us gods[a] who will go before us. As for this fellow Moses who brought us up out of Egypt, we don't know what has happened to him.'"- Exodus 32:1

The treaty between God and the chosen people ends with a rite. Moses has an altar erected in the midst of twelve tribes that represent the twelve tribes of Israel, that is, the twelve groups that descended from the sons of Jacob. On the altar are offered animals in the Holocaust (completely burned) and others in the sacrifice of communion (consumed by those present). The blood of the victims is sprinkled on the altar and sprinkled over the people to signify that, from this moment, God and Israel become consanguineous.

Then God calls Moses over the mountain and dictates other prescriptions concerning the cult. God orders Moses to build him a mobile sanctuary. God wants to live among his people; he wants a tent as a sign of his presence among those he loves. God orders his servant to also build an Ark in which the tablets of the law were to be kept. Then God establishes that Aaron and his sons, belonging to the tribe of Levi, are destined to perform the function of priests.

All these laws and prescriptions are gathered in the books of the Numbers, of Leviticus and of Deuteronomy which together with Genesis and Exodus make up the Pentateuch. This collection of five books therefore also takes the name of Legge (in Hebrew Toràh). While Moses speaks face to face with God, Israel is expected at the foot of Sinai. Moses is slow to descend. Israel then asks Aaron to build a base that was to represent the throne of God. Aaron, in good faith, thinking of doing something pleasing to God, to Moses and to the people, melts all the gold that Israel had brought from Egypt and had a throne built in the form of a calf. The golden calf, intended by Israel, did not want to portray a deity, an idol. And yet it resembled the idols of pagan peoples. Moses, having descended from the mountain, does not accept this throne, fearing that Israel will then make it an idol to worship. Angry, it shatters the tables of the law, destroys the golden calf and punishes the transgressors. Finally, Moses addresses this prayer to the God of Israel, a jealous God: *"Do not be angry with your people, O Lord."* Remember Abraham, Isaac, and Jacob and forgive your people. And God, in his infinite patience, listens to the prayer of Moses. It does not punish the people who have broken the main commandment of the alliance.

Traveling to Canaan

During the journey towards the oasis of Kades, south of Canaan, Israel experiences the protection of God in the desert. The peoples who inhabit those lands often oppose the march of Israel, but God, according to the agreements, always helps Israel to overcome that resistance. Israel's complaints, however, are not abating. The journey is prolonging beyond what was expected. Hunger and thirst put a strain on Israel. The people turned with the usual refrain against God and against Moses, *"Why did you make us come out of Egypt to make us die in this desert?* Here, there is neither bread nor water and we are sick of eating this manna. It is blank and too light. This time Jehovah harshly punishes Israel. Poisonous snakes bite numerous dying Israelites. Moses intervenes again in favor of the people and begs God to remove that insidious danger. God then orders Moses to build a copper serpent and place it on a pole. Anyone who looked at the copper snake after being bitten would remain alive. And so it happens. This episode also has a symbolic meaning. The copper serpent is a representation of the power and providence of God. God from evil himself knows how to obtain good. Whoever fixes his gaze on God runs no danger. Jesus, in the New Testament, will compare himself to the copper serpent. Whoever trusts Jesus and fixes his gaze on him, raised on the cross, will be saved. Israel continues its journey though still bedeviled with other obstacles and other tests.

Israel finally reaches the oasis of Kades. Moses sends some scouts to Canaan. They return excited and describe Canaan as a land where "milk and honey flows". Then Israel expects to the east of the Jordan River, in the territory of Transjordan.

The death of Moses

"Then Moses climbed Mount Nebo from the plains of Moab to the top of Pisgah, across from Jericho. There the Lord showed him the whole land—from Gilead to Dan, all of Naphtali, the territory of Ephraim and Manasseh, all the land of Judah as far as the Mediterranean Sea, the Negev and the whole region from the Valley of Jericho, the City of Palms, as far as Zoar. Then the Lord said to him, this is the land I promised on oath to Abraham, Isaac and Jacob

*when I said, 'I will give it to your descendants.' I have
let you see it with your eyes, but you will not cross
over into it.' And Moses the servant of the Lord died
there in Moab, as the Lord had said. He buried him
in Moab, in the valley opposite Beth Peor, but to this
day no one knows where his grave is. Moses was a
hundred and twenty years old when he died, yet his
eyes were not weak nor his strength gone. The
Israelites grieved for Moses in the plains of Moab
thirty days, until the time of weeping and mourning
was over."*- Deuteronomy 34:1-8

The king of that territory, realizing that he cannot
stop Israel by force tries to do it with magic. He sends
his most powerful magician, named Balaam, to Israel
because he solemnly curses the Jewish people. But
also Balaam is bent by the power of God. Instead of
cursing Israel, Balaam blesses him with these words:
Oracle of Balaam, son of Beor, and oracle of the man
with a penetrating eye. How beautiful are your tents,
O Israel? Who blesses you is blessed and who curses
you is cursed! The Promised Land is now a stone's
throw away. Just cross the Jordan River. But now the
time has come for Moses to be reunited with his
fathers, with Abraham, with Isaac and with Jacob.
After choosing Joshua as his successor, the old and
weary leader of Israel climbs a mountain to
contemplate the Promised Land.

From the top of Mount Nebo, beyond the Jordan,
Moses with his eyes embraces the country he

dreamed of for many years. Moses, for the last time, hears the firm and sweet voice of his God,

"This is the country" says the voice "for which I swore to Abraham, to Isaac and to Jacob. I will give it to your descendants. I showed it to you with your own eyes, but you will not enter it."

With this vision of Canaan in the eyes and with the certainty in his heart that the promises of God will come true, Moses falls asleep in the Lord. Thus the greatest prophet of Israel dies the leader, the liberator, the legislator, he who spoke face to face with God.

THE STORY OF JOSHUA AND THE JUDGES
(Joshua - Judges- Ruth)

PART 1
PASSAGE OF THE JORDAN - THE LAND OF CANAAN - THE FALL OF JERICHO - THE DEFEAT OF AI

The passage of the Jordan

"Early in the morning Joshua and all the Israelites set out from Shittim and went to the Jordan, where they camped before crossing over. After three days the officers went throughout the camp, giving orders to the people: 'When you see the ark of the covenant of the Lord your God, and the Levitical priests carrying it, you are to move out from your positions and follow it. Then you will know which way to go, since you have never been this way before. But keep a distance of about two thousand cubits between you and the ark; do not go near it.'"- Joshua 3:1-4

With Joshua the ancient promise made by God to Abraham, Isaac and Jacob are fulfilled. After forty years of deprivation and hardship in the desert, Israel now has before its eyes "the land where milk and honey flows". The Jordan River, like the Red Sea, is not just a geographical boundary, a religious frontier, a dimension of the spirit. The Jordan marks the end of a meaningless life and the beginning of a new life full of exciting perspectives. The crossing of the Jordan is a replica of the passage of the Red Sea. The waters open and the people cross the river at "dry feet". The priests dressed in sacred vestments, in the middle of the river support the Ark of the Covenant, while the people enter as solemnly as in a procession in the Promised Land. The description of the crossing of the river is symbolic. God himself, depicted by the waters of the Jordan, welcomes his people with open arms.

The people who enter the land of Canaan are young people, a generation born, tempered and purified by the difficulties of the desert. It is no longer a bunch of lawless slaves. Now Israel has the conscience of being a privileged people. Israel is divided into twelve tribes, but all linked by the same faith. One is their God: God. Only one is their leader: Joshua, son of Nun, of the tribe of Ephraim. After the people crossed the Jordan, Joshua had twelve slabs of stone collected from the riverbed and had they erected at the locality of Gilgal, east of Jericho. Then, addressing the people with his shrill voice, he says: - People of Israel! When your children ask you the meaning of these twelve stones you will say: In dry Israel has crossed this Jordan. God drained the waters as he did at the Red Sea. For all the peoples of the earth to know how strong the hand of the Lord is. Joshua causes all the males of Israel to be circumcised. And he too, as had already happened to

Abraham, Isaac, Jacob and Moses, hears the firm and sweet voice of God:

> *"Today," says the voice, "I have definitively removed from you the infamy of Egypt."*

The land of Canaan

Israel enters the land of Canaan around the year 1200 before Christ. At that time different peoples lived in that strip of land. The village is very small. It measures less than 230 kilometres and about 80 meters wide from north to south. Looks like the roof of a house. It rises gradually from the Mediterranean, reaches about a thousand meters of altitude and then descends rapidly to the Jordan Valley, which begins north over the Sea of Galilee and ends in the south with the Dead Sea.

At the time of Joshua, the Mediterranean coast is occupied to the north by the Phoenicians and to the south by the Philistines. The Phoenicians are merchants, while the Philistines, who already know the use of iron, are a warrior people from the Mediterranean islands. The Canaanites have lived in the centre of the town for centuries. The Canaanites are predominantly farmers, but they do not cultivate the whole earth. They had settled in some strategic locations and built fortified cities there. Around these cities, independent politically and militarily from each other, the peasants work some plot of land. The Canaanites worship numerous deities. In particular honour, they hold the goddess Ascera and the god Baal. To propitiate these deities, during their rituals, they even sacrifice human victims. Their shrines are built on the heights. Entering the land of Canaan, Israel must therefore necessarily clash against the interests of these peoples. The chosen people will above all have to face the Canaanites and the Philistines. The struggles will last for centuries and will be cruel and to death. They will cease with the last victories of King David over the Philistines around 1000 BC. The conquest of Canaan is described by the Bible in an epic form, with tones of exaggeration. These are heroic times for Israel and the settlement in Canaan is described in a heroic way. In reality, it has been more peaceful and less ruthless than it appears from the story of the battles and exterminations narrated in the books of Joshua and the Judges.

The fall of Jericho

"When the trumpets sounded, the army shouted, and at the sound of the trumpet, when the men gave a loud shout, the wall collapsed; so everyone charged straight in, and they took the city."- Joshua 6:20

An example of an epic style the Bible provides when describing the capture of Jericho, one of the fortified cities of the Canaanites, the first that Israel encounters as soon as it crosses the Jordan. Joshua is

114

a brilliant strategist, but above all, he is a man of faith.

While the women and children wait camped in Gilgal, Joshua with his men and accompanied by the priests carrying the Ark, arrives under the walls of Jericho. Joshua's army marched around the city walls for six days, playing the trumpets and carrying the Ark. The inhabitants of Jericho hear the sound of the cadenced march and the terrifying sound of the trumpets of Israel. On the seventh day, the walls of Jericho collapse and Israel triumphantly occupies the city. In reality, at the time of Joshua, the walls of Jericho were already in ruins. But within their perimeter, the Canaanites had settled. They flee terrified before the army of Joshua. The Israelites bypass the already crumbling walls and completely destroy the city.

The extermination of Jericho, and of other future Canaanite cities, is ordered by Joshua at the behest of God. Joshua fears that Israel will amalgamate with the Canaanites by adopting its customs and religion. The extermination of the conquered cities may seem cruel to a people who profess the commandment not to kill. But under certain circumstances, Joshua demands it to avoid dangerous contamination of his people. Such contaminations prove to be a real risk in later times. Israel, in fact, despite the warnings of its leaders, despite the law of the Covenant, will often adopt uses and customs of the Canaanites. Israel will even take on some pagan gods as its own, worshipping Ascera and Baal. God will then be very strict and punish his people. For the moment, God, the God of armies, is with Israel and fights at his side. God, we can say, that occupies the Promised Land for his people.

The defeat of Ai

"When the king of Ai saw this, he and all the men of the city hurried out early in the morning to meet Israel in battle at a certain place overlooking the Arabah. But he did not know that an ambush had been set against him behind the city. Joshua and all Israel let themselves be driven back before them, and they fled toward the wilderness. All the men of Ai were called to pursue them, and they pursued Joshua and were lured away from the city. Not a man remained in Ai or Bethel who did not go after Israel. They left the city open and went in pursuit of Israel."- Joshua 8:14-17

Only in one circumstance does Joshua's army suffer a bitter defeat. During the siege of the city of Ai, the Canaanites resist heroically, counterattack and annihilate a detachment of the army of Israel composed of three thousand men. The defeat is incomprehensible to Joshua. But immediately the cause is discovered. An Israelite, Achan, took possession of a part of the treasure destined for the treasure of the mobile sanctuary of Jahveh. Joshua punishes the transgressor with death and from that moment starts to win against his enemies. The punishment that God imparts to Israel because of the sin of one man indicates how God considers the responsibility of his people en bloc. The sin of one falls on everyone.

The sin of Achan is a bit the "re-edition" of Adam's sin, but it is also the "anticipation" of what will happen in the time of Jesus. How the sin of Adam falls on all of humanity and the sin of Achan falls on all of Israel, so the death of Jesus will save all the new people of God.

PART 2
THE CONQUEST OF CANAAN - THE DIVISION OF THE PROMISED LAND - THE ASSEMBLY OF SHECHEM - THE JUDGES OF ISRAEL

The conquest of Canaan

The conquest of Canaan is considered by the Bible as an exclusive work of God. The crossing of the Jordan and the fall of Jericho have a solemn, ritual, and almost liturgical cadences. The victory of Ai is also described as the work of Jehovah. God, when Israel remains faithful to the covenant, it fights and wins for him. The decisive help of God is also emphasized during the battle of Gibeon. Israel faces a powerful army. The Canaanites have joined forces with other peoples to oppose Israel. But Israel still wins. God disrupts the enemy army with a hailstorm of exceptional violence. However, the battle is not over even if the enemy is on the run. Now the night is coming.

With the favour of darkness the army of coalition peoples could reorganize. Then Joshua, in a ringing voice, commanded the sun, *"Oh sun, rest on Gibeon!"* And the sun, according to the biblical story, stops. Joshua has plenty of time to destroy the enemy army. Obviously, this episode is also symbolic. Not even God can stop the sun because the sun is already stationary with respect to the earth. At Gibeon the sun probably darkened, covered by a dense cloud or due to an eclipse. Then he returned to shine, giving the impression that the day started again. The Bible, reporting this episode, simply intends to affirm that God, and God alone, is the author of the victory of Gibeon.

The division of the Promised Land

"'As for all the inhabitants of the mountain regions from Lebanon to Misrephoth Maim, that is, all the Sidonians, I myself will drive them out before the Israelites. Be sure to allocate this land to Israel for an inheritance, as I have instructed you, 7 and divide it as an inheritance among the nine tribes and half of the tribe of Manasseh.'" - Joshua 13:6-7

After the battle of Gibeon, all the fortified cities of the Canaan surrender or fall into the hands of the Israelites. There are still some pockets of resistance, but now the land of Canaan is virtually in Israel's hands. The dangerous Philistines have always settled on the coast along the Mediterranean. But for the moment Israel does not care and does not care for them. The twelve tribes now have enough space to settle permanently in the Promised Land.

Thus, once the conquest is complete, Joshua divides the occupied land among the twelve tribes of Israel. The tribes of Gad and Ruben are established east of the Jordan. Then, starting from north to south, the tribes of Dan, Naphtali, Asher, Zebulun, Issachar, Ephraim, Benjamin, Judah and Simeon settle. The names of the tribes are the names of Jacob's sons or their children's children. Canaan is now the home of Israel.

The assembly of Shechem

"Then Joshua assembled all the tribes of Israel at Shechem. He summoned the elders, leaders, judges and officials of Israel, and they presented themselves before God."- Joshua 24:1

After assigning a territory to each tribe, Joshua now feels that his mission is about to end. Before dying, however, he intends to remind Israel of the pacts established with God. Israel has experienced God's faithfulness in keeping promises. God gave his people land and helped them with a "powerful hand and an outstretched arm". Now Israel solemnly promises God to be loyal to the pacts in turn. Joshua gathers the tribes of Israel to the city of Shechem. Before the assembled people, the conqueror of Canaan gives a memorable speech. It is his will and a summary of the wonderful works performed by God for his people. "Fear, therefore, God!" Joshua says with his voice still ringing.

"Serve it with integrity and loyalty. Do not serve the gods of this country, but God who brought you from the land of Egypt and gave you a land that you have not worked and cities that you have not built and vineyards and olive groves that you have not planted. Now choose who you want to serve: if the God of our fathers or the foreign gods of this country. As for me and my house, we want to serve the Lord."

His body is buried in the mountains in the territory of Ephraim. With the death of Joshua, the book of the Bible that bears his name ends. Throughout the life of Joshua, Israel remains faithful to God according to the promise made to Shechem.

The judges of Israel

During the assembly of Shechem, not only had Israel's alliance with God been renewed, but the foundations had also been laid for a social and political organization of the chosen people. The twelve tribes of Israel, despite being politically autonomous, forms a kind of confederation. At the head of every tribe are the elders of the people. In case of need all the tribes, or even just some of them, come together under the command of a single leader.

Unfortunately, after the death of Joshua, the chosen people, forgetting the promises of Shechem, let themselves be seduced by the Canaanite gods and worships Ascera and Baal. Then, God punishes his people and delivers them into the hands of the enemies, never completely tamed during the occupation of the Promised Land. When Israel is oppressed by enemies, it invokes its own God and converts to the covenant. God then arouses among the people charismatic figures, leaders, leaders who, with their heroic deeds, liberate Israel from their enemies.

These leaders, fortified and guided by God , are the "judges" of Israel and their amazing deeds are narrated in the book of the Bible that bears the title: The Judges. The number of judges presented by the Bible is conventional: twelve to remember the twelve tribes of Israel. Of these, only a few are considered "great" and among them stand the figures of Gideon and Samson.

PART 3
ISRAEL OPPRESSED BY THE MIDIANITES - GIDEON DEFEATS THE MIDIANITES - SAMSON: STRENGTH IN THE SERVICE OF GOD - RUTH, THE MOABITE

Israel oppressed by the Midianites

"Gideon sent messengers throughout the hill country of Ephraim, saying, 'Come down against the Midianites and seize the waters of the Jordan ahead of them as far as Beth Barah.'"- Judges 7:24

In the land of Midian, where Moses had taken refuge fleeing from Egypt and where Semite peoples lived, there also lived non-Semitic shepherds dedicated to the raid. These Midianites one day penetrate the land of Canaan where Israel has now settled. During their raids, the Midianites destroy, like a cloud of locusts, the products of the town. They didn't leave means of subsistence to Israel: neither sheep, nor oxen, nor donkeys, nor fruits of the soil. Israel is reduced to poverty because of the Midianites. The Israelites cry out to the Lord to be saved from those ruthless enemies. God then arouses in Israel a strong and valiant man because he frees the chosen people from the danger of the Midianites: this man is the judge Gideon, son of Joash, of the tribe of Manasseh.

Gideon defeats the Midianites

"So all the men of Ephraim were called out and they seized the waters of the Jordan as far as Beth Barah. They also captured two of the Midianite leaders, Oreb and Zeeb. They killed Oreb at the rock of Oreb, and Zeeb at the winepress of Zeeb. They pursued the Midianites and brought the heads of Oreb and Zeeb to Gideon, who was by the Jordan."- Judges 7:24-25

The Midianites are camped in the land of Cancan near the Jordan River. Gideon summons the best fighters of the tribes of Israel. Warriors from the tribes of Manasseh, Asher, Zebulun, and Naphtali arrive. With this army, consisting of thirty-two thousand men, Gideon camps south of the Midianite positions and prepares for the attack. While the army of Israel is waiting for the signal of battle, so God speaks to Judge Gideon,

"The people who are with you are too numerous. Israel could boast before me and say: My hand has saved me. Now you announce in front of everyone: Anyone who is afraid and trembles goes back."

Gideon puts his warriors to the test according to the command of God. Twenty-two a thousand men come back and ten thousand remains. God tells Gideon, *"People are still too numerous."* Get them down to the river and how many people will lick the water with their tongue, as they touch the dog, you will put them aside. And how many to drink they will bring the water to the mouth with the hand, those you will choose. Gideon does as God commanded him, and the men who drink bringing their water to their mouth with their hands are three hundred. Then God says to Gideon:

> *"With these three hundred men I will save you and put the Midianites in your hands."*

Gideon divides the three hundred men into three ranks, gives trumpets and torches to all, and then gives them these instructions: - When I play the trumpet, you will also play your trumpets and shout. Then we will fall with torches lit in the field of Midian. When the three hundred men rush into the curtains of the Midianites during the night, these, terrified by that noise and by the torches wandering in the dark, flee in hurry trembling and shouting and disperse. The Midianites escape like a cloud of locusts in front of the fire. The Midianites abandon the land of Canaan forever. Israel, once again, is safe because God fought at his side with "a powerful hand and an outstretched arm."

Samson: strength at the service of God

"The woman gave birth to a boy and named him Samson. He grew and the Lord blessed him, 25 and the Spirit of the Lord began to stir him while he was in Mahaneh Dan, between Zorah and Eshtaol." - Judges 13:24-25

The years go by. Israel spends periods of relative tranquility alternating with periods of distress and struggle. From time to time the chosen people let themselves be seduced by foreign gods and then God punishes them by putting them in the hands of his enemies. Israel repents and cries to the Lord and the Lord sends a judge to free the people. The last of the great judges of Israel is Samson, whose name means "man of the sun". Samson must face very brave and formidably armed enemies: the Philistines who live along the Mediterranean coast near Gaza. The Philistines know how to forge iron, while Israel still uses swords and bronze spears.

Since he was a child, Samson has consecrated himself to the Lord with the vow of the Nazariteship which consists of not shaving his hair and beard and abstaining from intoxicating drinks. Samson, who is endowed with powerful muscles, in many circumstances, disturbs and mocks the Philistines. But one day the judge consecrated to God falls in love with a Philistine woman: Delilah. With caresses, the woman manages to understand the secret of Samson's strength: a force that does not derive from the judge from the powerful musculature, but from his consecration to God. One night, while Samson is immersed in sleep, Delilah makes him shave his hair and binds it firmly. Samson's strength fades instantly. Not because he is tied to his hair, but because he, revealing his secret to Delilah, has betrayed the vow and God, therefore, abandons him to himself. The

Philistines easily capture Samson, dig out his eyes and chain him to a millstone.

After sometimes, however, Samson repents of his sin. He understands that he cannot trust his own muscles, but only the help of the Lord. He renews his vow and, as his hair grows back, the Lord restores his strength and courage. One day the Philistines lead the prisoner to their temple to have fun behind him. All the Philistine leaders are gathered in the temple. Samson tells the boy who is holding his hand:

"Let me touch the columns on which the house rests so that I can lean on them."

Samson palpates the two middle columns; then, after invoking the Lord, he bends with all his strength pushing one column with the right and the other with the left. The house ruins the leaders and all the people inside it. With his death Samson causes more enemies to die than he killed during his life. Once again Israel is safe because God helped him "with a powerful hand and an outstretched arm." The book of Judges closes with the exploits of Samson. It is a book that is a hymn to the patience of God towards Israel. After the death of Joshua, the chosen people began to walk along a slope that leads to increasingly serious infidelities. Israel has a short memory and a hard brain. He soon forgets the benefits of God and trusts only in his own strength. The ancient sin of Adam resurfaces. But God is always stronger than man's sin. Despite Israel's stubbornness, the Lord with inexhaustible patience and infinite mercy carries out his project of salvation.

Ruth, the Moabite

"At this they wept aloud again. Then Orpah kissed her mother-in-law goodbye, but Ruth clung to her."- Ruth 1:14

During the period of the Judges, among many battles and heroic deeds, the Bible narrates an episode full of sweetness and poetry. It is the story of Ruth, a young foreigner, a Moabite. The land of Moab is east of the Dead Sea. The story of Ruth occupies an entire book, although very short, of the Bible. At the time of the Judges, therefore, a Jewish family immigrated to the land of Moab because a famine struck the land of Canaan. The young Mahlon, belonging to this Jewish family, marries Ruth, a beautiful Moabite with very sweet eyes, large and velvety like those of a doe. Unfortunately, however, Mahlon dies and Rut is still a very young widow.

Mahlon's mother and Ruth's mother-in-law, old Naomi, decides to return to Israel. Naomi tells Ruth,

"You better stay in your land because in my country you would be considered an enemy and a foreigner."
But Ruth, in a firm voice, answers her mother-in-law, "Where you go, I'll go too; where you'll stop, I'll stop. Your people will be my people; your God will be my God. Where you die, I too will die and I will be buried. Only death will separate me from you."

So as not to abandon old Naomi, Ruth, therefore, leaves the land of her fathers, leaves her tongue and loved ones, leaves her gods and entrusts herself to the unknown God of Israel. Naomi and Ruth, hand in hand, come after many days of travel in the land of Canaan. Naomi finds her friends, but Ruth knows no one. To help the old mother-in-law who is very poor, Ruth goes to glean the barley in the fields of Booz, a rich and gentle young Jew. Every day Ruth walks behind Boaz's harvesters and picks up the leftovers of the ears inside her apron.

One morning Boaz arrives in the camp where Ruth is gleaning and asks her servant: "Who is this young woman?" The servant replies, "It is a Moabite, the one who returned with Naomi from the Moab campaign." Boaz tells Ruth, "Don't go gleaning in another camp, but stay here." When you are thirsty, go and drink from the jars of my reapers. Ruth, red-faced with emotion, prostrates with her face to the ground and tells Boaz, "Why have I found grace before your eyes, I who am a foreigner?" Boaz replies, "I was told how much you did for your mother-in-law after your husband's death and how you abandoned your father, your mother and your country to come to a people you didn't know before. The Lord, under whose wings you have come to take refuge, you repay yourself for what you have done."

Then, at the time of the meal, Boaz tells her, *"Come and eat with me* - and hands her some toasted grain. Ruth eats it fully and sets aside a little to take it to

Naomi. Boaz says to his reapers, ***"Drop some ears of barley for her when you harvest."*** Abandon them, so that it may collect them. That evening Rut returns to the old Naomi and delivers the whole harvest as usual without holding a barley grain for herself. He also hands the bundle with the leftovers from the meal to Noemi. His attachment to his mother-in-law, his altruism, is rewarded by God.

Young Boaz falls in love with Ruth and marries her. Thus the young Moabite, who arrived in Canaan very poor and rich only in her great heart, becomes one of the most envied women in the country. The story of Ruth shows that love is never useless and eventually rewards those who exercise it gently, humbly, with dedication, with frankness, with simplicity. These are, in fact, the qualities that God requires of any man to assure him of his protection and his benevolence.

THE STORY OF THE KINGS (1 AND 2 SAMUEL – 1 KINGS 1-13)

PART 1
ISRAEL DREAMS OF THE MONARCHY - THE VOCATION OF SAMUEL - ISRAEL CALLS FOR A KING - SAUL FIRST KING OF ISRAEL

Israel dreams of the monarchy

"So all the elders of Israel gathered together and came to Samuel at Ramah. They said to him, 'you are old, and your sons do not follow your ways; now appoint a king to lead us, such as all the other nations have.'"- 1 Samuel 8:4-5

After the experience of the Judges, Israel becomes aware that only the stable union of the twelve tribes can save it from enemies. The whole land of Canaan is now firmly in the hands of the chosen people except for that band along the Mediterranean occupied by the terrible and aggressive Philistines. Israel, confronting the neighbouring peoples all in a monarchical regime, now dreams of having a king, a ruler who governs the entire nation, who leads a duly trained army to the final victory over the Philistines and any other external enemy. From the Federation of the tribes, Israel wants to move to the monarchy. Until now God

132

was considered not only the only God but also the political leader of Israel.

Now it seems to put aside. Israel seems to trust more than one flesh-and-blood king, then his God, the King of armies. The Sinai alliance solemnly renewed at Shechem in the time of Joshua seems to be definitively set aside. The infidelities against God multiply. Israel increasingly turns to Canaanite gods, to Baal and Ascera. The chosen people continue to walk along that slope that takes them farther and farther away from their God. The people of God, the holy and jealous God, the people forged by Moses, the people heir to the promises made to Abraham, Isaac and Jacob are degrading; he is heading towards decline and catastrophe. The man called by God to manage Israel's troubled passage from the regime founded on the Federation of the tribes to the monarchic regime is Samuel.

The vocation of Samuel

Samuel is a judge of Israel, a priest and a prophet. Like all the great characters of the Old Testament, he is called directly by God to carry out the difficult mission of choosing a king for Israel. Since he was a child, Samuel has been entrusted to the care of a holy priest named Eli. Eli worshipped God in the temple-sanctuary of Silo, where the Ark of the Covenant was kept. One night the young Samuel hears a firm and sweet voice: - *Samuel!* - says the voice. The boy promptly replies, *"Here I am!"* Then he runs to the

133

old Eli who rests in the next room and tells him: - You called me, here I am. Eli replies, *"I didn't call you, go back to sleep."* A second and a third time Samuel is called and always runs to Eli. Finally, Eli realizes that it is the Lord who calls the young man and tells him, *"Go away to sleep* and, if he calls you again, you will say: Speak, Lord, because your servant is listening to you."

When Samuel hears the firm and sweet voice for the fourth time, he answers as Eli advised him. The Lord then gives the young Samuel the mission to speak on his behalf to the chosen people to advise and admonish and correct.

Israel asks for a king

Samuel carries out the mission that God has entrusted to him with great firmness. Soon his fame spread among the twelve tribes of Israel. Meanwhile, the Philistines are becoming more and more threatening. With their iron weapons, they seem unbeatable. During a battle, they even manage to take over the Ark of the Covenant. Then the chiefs of the tribes turn to the prophet Samuel and tell him: - Establish for us a king who will govern us, as happens for all peoples. To Samuel the request seems bad, therefore he prays to the Lord and the Lord answers him: - Listen to the voice of the people. They want to reject me because I do not reign over them. Listen also to their request, but warn them about the claims of the king who will reign over them. Samuel, in a voice full of sadness, tells Israel,

"The king you want will treat you harshly."

He will take your children and send them to his wagons. He will force them to plough his fields and harvest his crops. He will also take your daughters to make them cooks and bakers. He will confiscate your herds, and then you will cry to the Lord because of the king you want to elect, but the Lord will not listen to you. In vain, Samuel paints the behaviour of the eventual future king in bleak tones. In vain he tries to defend the cause of God. The people don't listen to him and he insists: - No, there is a king over us. We too will be like all peoples. The king will come out to our head and fight our battles. The Lord then says resigned to his prophet,

"Listen to them, Samuel! A king reigns over them."

And the voice of God is imbued with a pang of infinite sadness.

Saul first king of Israel

"Samuel said to all the people, 'Do you see the man the Lord has chosen? There is no one like him among all the people.' Then the people shouted, 'Long live the king!'"- 1 Samuel 10:24

The first king of Israel is Saul, son of Kish, of the tribe of Benjamin. Saul has no quality to reign. He is nervous and short-tempered. It's just beautiful and tall. It's all appearance. Overcome any other Israelite from your shoulders. Saul is chosen because Israel remains disappointed and trusts only in God. One day, therefore, Saul meets Samuel by chance and he, inspired by God, understands that the choice fell on this tall and handsome young man. Samuel takes an ampoule of oil and pours it, according to the use of time, on Saul's head to consecrate him king: - Here, - says Samuel - the Lord has anointed you head on Israel his people. You will have power over the people and you will release them from the hands of the enemies. Only a part of the tribes of Israel accepts the king chosen by God. Some tribes reserve the right to decide later, based on the exploits that the new king would have performed. Saul is quite brave in battle and, in several clashes; he beats the Philistines even if he cannot defeat them definitively. But Saul is not very respectful towards God and the prophet Samuel. One day he claims rights that belong only to priests. He offers a sacrifice to God to obtain a victory. Samuel then rebuked him and said to him:

"You have rejected the word of the Lord, and he has rejected you as king."

In vain does Saul beg for forgiveness? Samuel does not even listen to him and goes away indignantly. Saul then takes Samuel's cloak to hold him. A corner of the mantle tears and the prophet says to Saul with contempt:

> **"The Lord has taken the kingdom from your hands, as you have torn my cloak."**

Then Samuel leaves without turning around, leaving the king dismayed. For a long time Saul stands as if he were dazed, turning that piece of cloth between his hands.

PART 2
DAVID IS ANOINTED KING -
THE CHALLENGE OF GOLIATH
- DAVID BRINGS DOWN
GOLIATH

David is anointed king

"So David went up there with his two wives, Ahinoam of Jezreel and Abigail, the widow of Nabal of Carmel. David also took the men who were with him, each with his family, and they settled in Hebron and its towns. Then the men of Judah came to Hebron, and there they anointed David king over the tribe of Judah."- 2 Samuel 2:2-4

God tells his prophet Samuel: - Fill your horn and parts with oil. I order you to go to Bethlehem from Jesse, from the tribe of Judah. Among the sons of Jesse, you will choose the new king of Israel and anoint him. Samuel goes to Jesse's house and asks the old patriarch to show him his children. While Samuel reviews them, he feels the voice of God within him, "Do not look at their appearance, because I do not look at what the man looks at. Man looks at the appearance, I look at the heart." Samuel understands that none of the sons of

Jesse present is the one designated by God to reign over Israel. Then Samuel asks Jesse, "Are all your children here?" Jesse replies, "No, it remains the smallest that is now grazing the flock. His name is David." "Send for him!" orders Samuel.

When the young David is before Samuel, he understands that he is the one designated by the Lord. Then, the prophet takes the horn of oil and consecrates King David among his brothers. God chooses David because he is the smallest of the brothers. The Lord, to show that every good comes from him, always prefers small and insignificant things to carry out his plan of salvation.

The Goliath Challenge

"Goliath stood and shouted to the ranks of Israel, 'why do you come out and line up for battle? Am I not a Philistine, and are you not the servants of Saul? Choose a man and have him come down to me. If he is able to fight and kill me, we will become your subjects; but if I overcome him and kill him, you will become our subjects and serve us.'"- 1 Samuel 17:8-9

For the time being David is not officially proclaimed king. Samuel fears Saul's reaction and advises young David to stay at Saul's court as a simple page. Saul also becomes fond of David because he is a skilled zither player and the music had the magical power to calm Saul's nervousness. Meanwhile, the Philistines are becoming more and more threatening. They gather a new army and camp near Saul's tents. A sample called Goliath comes out of the Philistine camp. He is more than two meters tall. It is covered with bronze plate armour. He has a helmet on his head and bronze greaves on his legs. It has a spear with an iron tip and an enormous sword, also of iron. And a perfect war machine. He stops in front of the hosts of Israel and shouts to them with a voice that resembles thunder: "Why did you go out and take sides in battle? I am a philistine and you are the vile servants of Saul. Choose a man among you who fights against me. If it strikes me, we will be your slaves. If I break it down, you will be our slaves. The army of Israel under Saul's command is terrified by the presence of this giant with the voice similar to thunder. No Israelite warrior dares to accept the challenge.

Then David, who is in the camp of Israel, makes Saul this proposal: - I will go to fight against this Philistine. Saul smiles ironically at David's boldness and tells him:

"You cannot go against this Philistine."

You are a boy and he has been a man of arms since his youth. But David tells Saul: - *The Lord will help me against this Philistine*. Saul then, perhaps envying the trust that David shows in the Lord, says to the boy:

"Well, go and the Lord be with you."

David brings down Goliath

"So David triumphed over the Philistine with a sling and a stone; without a sword in his hand he struck down the Philistine and killed him. David ran and stood over him. He took hold of the Philistine's sword and drew it from the sheath. After he killed him, he cut off his head with the sword."- 1 Samuel 17:50-51

Saul dresses David with his own armour. He puts a bronze helmet on his head and puts on his armour. Then David encircles Saul's sword over his armour but tries in vain to walk. Then he tells Saul: "I can't walk with all this stuff on." I'm not used. David frees himself of his armour, takes his shepherd's stick in his hand, chooses five smooth pebbles from the stream and places them in his bag. He still takes his sling in his hand and moves towards the Philistine. Goliath advances step by step closer to David and, with every step taken by the giant, it seems that the earth is shaking. The Philistine scrutinizes David and has contempt for him because he is a boy. He gets to his belt, yes and no. He shouts to him: "Am I a dog, why do you come to me with a stick?" And his voice resembles that of thunder. David, not afraid of that mountain of bronze-clad flesh, says calmly: *"You come to me with the breastplate, with the spear and the sword."* I come to you in the name of God, Lord of hosts, and God of the hosts of Israel whom you have insulted. On this same day, the Lord will make you fall into my hands. I'll break you down and I'll take your head off your body. The whole earth will

141

know that there is a God in Israel. - Call to talk! - Says Goliath sure as a lion annoyed by a gnat - come forward and I will give your meat to the birds of the sky. David calmly throws his hand into the bag, takes a stone from it and throws it with the sling against the Philistine. The stone hisses in the air and penetrates the Philistine's forehead just at the helpless point. Goliath, with a crash of scrap metal, falls with his face to the ground. David makes a jump and is above the Philistine. He takes his sword, draws it and kills him. Then, holding the heavy and sharp weapon in both hands, with that size the giant's head is clear. The Philistines saw that their champion is dead and they flee. The same iron the sword that had been the pride of Goliath becomes the instrument of his death. Little David once again demonstrated that salvation comes only from the Lord.

PART 3

DAVID AND JONATHAN - THE KINGDOM OF DAVID - THE SIN OF DAVID - SOLOMON BECOME KING

David and Jonathan

"Saul told his son Jonathan and all the attendants to kill David. But Jonathan had taken a great liking to David and warned him, 'My father Saul is looking for a chance to kill you. Be on your guard tomorrow morning; go into hiding and stay there. I will go out and stand with my father in the field where you are. I'll speak to him about you and will tell you what I find out.'"- 1 Samuel 19:1-3

After the victory over Goliath, little David appears before Saul. Next, to the throne of Saul there is also the son Jonathan who, on the death of his father, according to the use of dynastic monarchies, would have inherited the throne. As soon as Jonathan sees David, he feels bound to him by a great friendship. The two are about the same age. Jonathan removes the cloak she is wearing and gives it to David and adds his sword, bow and belt. The people of Israel also pay tribute to David. The women dance in front of him and sing,

"Saul killed a thousand warriors, but David killed ten thousand." Saul is very irritated and those words seem bad to him. He says to himself:

"They gave David ten thousand and they gave me only one thousand. He lacks nothing but the throne ".

From that day on, Saul becomes jealous of David and begins to persecute him. Once while David plays the lyre, Saul holds the spear thinking*: "*Now I'll nail David to the wall!" He throws the weapon, but David manages to dodge it by a whisker. Then he decides to run away and hide. But Saul pursues him with the army and tries to kill him. On this occasion, Jonathan informs his friend, saying: *"Be on guard."* I will talk to my father on your behalf. Even in other circumstances, David manages to save himself thanks to his friend's help. Yet Jonathan has every interest in making David die. He knows that David is loved by God and by the people and can become king in his place. However, Jonathan is ready to give up the throne in order to help his friend. Jonathan's loyalty is reciprocated by David.

One day David could have killed Saul, but he merely cut a piece of his cloak with his sword. Another time he could have nailed Saul to the ground with his spear. But he spares the king's life from the affection that Jonathan showed him. Even David has the interest that Saul dies. He would have finished fleeing and hiding and the people would have

144

proclaimed him king, confirming God's choice. But David does not take revenge because he has a noble heart and for the friendship that binds him to Jonathan. When Jonathan and Saul died at the hands of the Philistines during a battle, David weeps bitterly: Why did the heroes fall in the battle? Jonathan, for your death I feel pain, anguish hugs me, my brother, Jonathan! You were very dear to me! Your friendship was precious to me. Thus David weeps over the heights of Gilboa, before the remains of the first king of Israel and his friend Jonathan.

The kingdom of David

With the death of Saul, David is proclaimed king by all the tribes of Israel. Meanwhile, the prophet Samuel dies. His mission is now complete. Israel is now a united kingdom. David, a king dear to the heart of God, re-conquers the Ark of the Covenant and definitively defeats the Philistines. Then he establishes his palace in Jerusalem. The city located on the hill of Zion becomes the capital of the kingdom of Israel; becomes the city of David. The king with great honours and celebrations transports the Ark into the city. While the Ark of the Lord triumphantly enters Jerusalem, David dances before it with joy. Jerusalem becomes the city of God, the holy city. David, to honour God who has granted him many victories, thinks of building a splendid temple in the holy city to his God. But the prophet Nathan, who lives near the palace of David, says to the king:

145

- The Lord does not want a house. He has always lived in a tent since Israel came out of Egypt. The Lord will instead make a home for you. He will make your throne stable forever. Your kingdom will never end. Nathan's prophecy will come true. The throne of David, of the tribe of Judah, will one day be inherited by the Savior. Jesus, of the lineage of David, will not ascend the throne of his illustrious ancestor according to the flesh. Jesus, the saviour, will reign in the hearts of the men who will accept him. And his kingdom will never end.

David- the sin of David

Unfortunately, in his old age, even David behaves badly before the eyes of God. He falls in love with a married woman and, in order to have her, he makes her husband die. The prophet Nathan reproaches, in the name of God, the great king of Israel: - There were two men - says the prophet - who lived in the same city. One was rich and the other poor. The rich man had much cattle; the poor man had only a little sheep he had raised with such tenderness. A passing guest arrived at the rich man's house and these, instead of taking a sheep from his flocks to offer a meal to the guest, stole the poor man's sheep and prepared a dish for it. In hearing this story, David lights up with anger and exclaims: - For the life of the Lord, the man who did this deserves death. - You are that man! - Then says Nathan with a harsh voice and an index finger pointing at the king -. You stole your wife from your subject to make her your bride. My story was just a parable, an example, to make you understand the gravity of your sin.

Then David, with his eyes lowered and his face red with shame, confesses to Nathan: *"I have truly sinned against the Lord."* Have mercy on me, O God. Nathan realizes that David is sincerely repentant and replies: - The Lord, in his mercy, has forgiven your sin. God forgives King David, while he had refused to forgive Saul who had committed a lesser sin. But David's repentance is sincere, while Saul's had been dictated by fear. God, as Jesus will teach, is willing to forgive even very serious sins, when repentance starts from the heart. To those who love a lot - Jesus will say - a lot will be forgiven.

Solomon become king

However David, during his last years, will have to suffer a lot. One of his sons, Absalom, rebels against him and David is forced to defend himself. David's army chases Absalom. David had ordered his soldiers not to kill the rebel, but to capture him alive. Absalom tries to escape from her father's soldiers. He runs away riding a mule. The animal enters under the branches of a tree and Absalom remains entangled in the branches for the hair. One of David's soldiers then takes the bow and dips three darts, one after the other, into the heart of Absalom.

When David is informed of the death of his son, he cries bitter tears, as he had cried before the remains of Saul and Jonathan. Covering his face with his hands, old David sobs desperately: *"My son Absalom!"* Assault, my son! My son! And nobody can comfort him. David, before his death, names his son Solomon as his successor. The throne would have belonged to Adonijah, the eldest of the sons of David.

Instead, the king chooses the young Solomon, following the same logic of God who prefers the little ones. Nathan pours oil on Solomon's head, according to usage. From that moment on Solomon becomes the new king of Israel. Feeling close to the day of his own death, David makes these recommendations to his son Solomon: ***"I go down the road of every man on earth."*** Be strong and be a man. Keep the law of the Lord and execute its commands. After forty years of reigning, David falls asleep with his fathers and is buried in Jerusalem, his city, the holy city.

PART 4

THE WISDOM OF SOLOMON - THE TEMPLE - THE DIVISION OF THE KINGDOM

The wisdom of Solomon

" 'Now, Lord my God, you have made your servant king in place of my father David. But I am only a little child and do not know how to carry out my duties. Your servant is here among the people you have chosen, a great people, too numerous to count or number. So give your servant a discerning heart to govern your people and to distinguish between right and wrong. For who is able to govern this great people of yours?' "- 1 Kings 3:7-9

At the beginning of the reign, Solomon shows himself worthy of the paternal choice. David had unified Israel and established Jerusalem as the capital bringing the Ark of the Covenant to it. The glory of Solomon is linked instead to the construction in Jerusalem of the "house of God ", the temple. Before making the construction of the temple, Solomon offers God numerous sacrifices at the heights of Gibeon. In Gibeon, the Lord appears to Solomon in a dream during the night and tells him: - Ask me what I must grant you. And Solomon says: - Lord, you have made me reign in the place of David, my father. Well, I am a boy; I don't know how to regulate myself. Give me a docile heart so that I can do justice to your people and know how to distinguish well from evil. The Lord likes that Solomon asked for wisdom and tells him:

"Because you asked for wisdom and did not ask for long life or wealth for you, behold, I grant you a wise and intelligent heart. And I grant you also what you have not asked for, that is, wealth and glory and I will also prolong your life".

In many circumstances, Solomon shows that he possesses a wise and intelligent heart. One day, for example, two mothers with the same right on children are presented by the king. One of them says: - Listen to me, sir. This other woman and I have had a child. But this woman's son died during the night because she lay down on it and suffocated him. She got up in the middle of the night, took my son from my side and put her dead son next to me. The other woman says: - It's not true! My son is the living one, yours is the dead one. The king orders: - Take me a sword! They carry a sword in the presence of the king. Then Solomon commands: - Cut the living son in two and give one half at one and one half at the other woman. Then, the mother of the living son says all frightened: - Lord, give her the living child, but do not kill him! The other says with indifference: *"Don't be mine or yours."* Divide it into two as well. Solomon then takes the floor and concludes: - Give the first woman the living child. That's her mother.

The temple

"You know that because of the wars waged against my father David from all sides, he could not build a temple for the Name of the Lord his God until the Lord put his enemies under his feet. But now the Lord my God has given me rest on every side, and there is no adversary or disaster. I intend, therefore, to build a temple for the Name of the Lord my God, as the Lord told my father David, when he said, 'Your son whom I will put on the throne in your place will build the temple for my Name.'"- 1 Kings 5:3-5

Around the year 960 BC, about 250 years after Israel's entry into the land of Canaan, Solomon begins the construction of the temple in Jerusalem. The plan of the temple follows that of the mobile tent that God had raised in the desert in the time of Moses. The temple is about 40 meters long, 10 meters wide and 15 meters high. In front, there is a large atrium where two magnificent bronze columns rise. An inner courtyard called the Saint follows. In the courtyard rise ten candlesticks of pure gold. Also in the courtyard, there is a bronze basin with water for ablutions. In addition, there is an altar where incense is burned. Twelve loaves of the twelve tribes of Israel are perennially placed on a table.

Occasionally the bread is renewed. The innermost chamber of the temple is the Holy of Holies. A precious veil divides the Saint from the Holy of Holies. In the Holy of Holies, where only the high priest can enter, the Ark of the Covenant is placed which contains the tablets of the law. The temple walls inside are all lined with cedar wood laminated with gold. The construction of the temple lasts twenty years. In the end, Solomon proceeds to solemn dedication to God. For that circumstance, Solomon addresses a prayer to God: - Lord, God of Israel, there is no God like you, neither up there in the heavens, nor down here on earth. You keep the covenant and the mercy with your servants who walk before you. Listen, O God, to my prayer. May your eyes be open night and day to this house that I dedicate to you today from the day of dedication the temple becomes the centre of worship, the heart of Jerusalem, as the holy city is the heart of the kingdom of Israel.

The division of the kingdom

Unfortunately, King Solomon did not appear very wise during his old age. He falls in love with some foreign women who attract him to their gods. To please the women of whom he is in love, Solomon follows and honours the goddess of the city of Sidon and the god of the people of the Ammonites and the god of the Moabites. Therefore, the Lord is indignant against Solomon and tells him in a firm voice: "Because you have behaved like this and have not kept my covenant, I will tear the kingdom away from you and deliver it to your subject." But not the whole kingdom will tear you away. I will give one part to your son Rehoboam for the sake of David my servant and for the love of Jerusalem, the city I chose. Shortly thereafter, a court official named Jeroboam, of the tribe of Ephraim rebels against the king. And God is with him. Jeroboam one day meets the prophet Achia on the street wearing a new cloak. They are just the two of them in the open countryside. Achia grabs the new cloak he is wearing and tears it into twelve pieces. Then he says to Jeroboam: -

Take ten pieces, because the Lord gives you ten tribes of the kingdom. Only two tribes will remain with Solomon and his descendants.

The glorious reign of Solomon breaks in two on the death of the king who, despite his wisdom, had been unfaithful to the alliance. Rehoboam, son of Solomon, will reign over two tribes: Judah and Benjamin. Jeroboam will reign over the remaining ten. The reign of Rehoboam, or kingdom of Judah, or kingdom of the south, has as its capital Jerusalem. The kingdom of Jeroboam, or kingdom of Ephraim, or kingdom of the north, has as its capital Samaria. Even the history of Israel from this moment is divided into two. The monarchy has failed. God has made Israel experience firsthand that human kingdoms cannot resist if they turn away from justice, from the truth, from faith. But just when everything seems lost, God, in his infinite patience, still tries to recover his northern and southern kingdoms to his alliance. God will send his prophets into the two kingdoms because, speaking on his behalf, they warn the kings and the people and lead them back to him.

THE STORY OF THE PROPHETS (1 KINGS 14-22 - 2 KINGS - PROPHETIC BOOKS)

PART 1
GOD IS GOD - NO ONE LISTENS TO THE PROPHETS - AMOS AND HOSEA - THE PROPHETS OF THE KINGDOM OF JUDAH

God is God

Eighteen kings succeed one another in the kingdom of Ephraim and one is more corrupt than the other. That distance the people from the worship and the law of God. At the time of King Ahab, the cult of Baal became official. In the kingdom, there are no more priests than God, but only priests of Baal. God then raises a passionate defender in the northern kingdom: Elijah, the prophet of fire. The name of Elijah means "God is God". Elijah meets King Ahab, unfaithful and sacrilege, and tells him: - You are the ruin of Israel! And the prophet's voice resembles the hiss of a whip.

Ahab is full of pride and presumption, but the prophet of God does not fear: - The true God is God and I will prove it to you. I challenge you in front of all the people. Gather your 450 priests of Baal to Mount Carmel. They will invoke Baal, but he will not listen. While the God of Israel, my God, will not remain silent and will manifest. The people of the kingdom of Ephraim are gathered on Mount Carmel. On one side there are 450 priests of Baal, smiling, confident. They prance themselves in the precious hangings of their cult. On the other hand, there is the prophet Elijah, alone. Wear a long cloak. He has a frown and long hair ruffled by the wind.

Elijah approaches the people and says in a sharp voice: *"How long will you limp with two feet?"* If God is God, follow him! If it is Baal, follow him! Embarrassed people remain silent. Elijah continues: - I remained alone as a prophet of God, while the prophets of Baal is 450. Well, give us two bullocks. They choose one, the squartino, and place it on the wood without setting it on fire. I will prepare the other bullock and put it on the wood without setting it on fire. You will invoke the name of your god and I will invoke the name of God. The divinity that will respond by granting fire is God! All the people respond: - The proposal is good.

The priests of Baal prepare the altar with the quartered bullock. Then they invoke the name of Baal from morning until noon. They go around the altar, they jump, they shout at the top of their lungs: "Baal, answer us!" Answer us, Baal! But you don't hear a breath or an answer. They continue to jump more and more excited and shout louder and louder.

Elijah, with arms crossed, makes fun of them and says: - Cry out louder, because he is a god! Maybe he's lost in thought, or he's busy in some business, or maybe he's on a journey ... If he's ever asleep, he'll wake up. Shout out, shout louder. But from Baal, there is no response, nor a sign of attention.

Elijah then commands all the people: - Come closer! And his voice resembles the hiss of a whip. Elijah builds the altar, digs around a small canal, and arranges the wood and the quartered bullock. Then he says: - Fill four jugs of water and pour them on the victim and on the wood. Do this three times. Water flows around the altar and even the Canaletto fills with water. Then Elijah, in a ringing voice, dresses her and her hair ruffled by the wind, says: - God, Lord, and God of Abraham, of Isaac and of Jacob! Today we know that you are the God of Israel and that I am your prophet! Answer me, Lord, and let the people know that you are the only true God! Convert, O Lord, their hearts! As soon as Elijah finishes this prayer, a globe of fire falls on the altar and consumes the victim and the wood and the stones in an instant and dries all the water of the canal. To this view all prostrate themselves with their faces to the ground and exclaim: - God is God! God is God!

No one listens to the prophets

Eighteen kings succeed one another in the kingdom of Ephraim and one is more corrupt than the other. That distances the people from the worship and the law of God. At the time of King Ahab, the cult of Baal became official. In the kingdom, there are no more priests than God, but only priests of Baal. God then raises a passionate defender in the northern kingdom: Elijah, the prophet of fire. The name of Elijah means "God is God". Elijah meets King Ahab, unfaithful and sacrilege, and tells him: - You are the ruin of Israel! And the prophet's voice resembles the hiss of a whip.

Ahab is full of pride and presumption, but the prophet of God does not fear: - The true God is God and I will prove it to you. I challenge you in front of all the people. Gather your 450 priests of Baal to Mount Carmel. They will invoke Baal, but he will not listen. While the God of Israel, my God, will not remain silent and will manifest. The people of the kingdom of Ephraim are gathered on Mount Carmel. On one side there are 450 priests of Baal, smiling, confident. They prance themselves in the precious hangings of their cult. On the other hand, there is the prophet Elijah, alone. Wear a long cloak. He has a frown and long hair ruffled by the wind.

Elijah approaches the people and says in a sharp voice: "How long will you limp with two feet?" If God is God, follow him! If it is Baal, follow him! Embarrassed people remain silent. Elijah continues: - I remained alone as a prophet of God, while the prophets of Baal is 450. Well, give us two bullocks. They choose one, the squartino, and place it on the wood without setting it on fire. I will prepare the other bullock and put it on the wood without setting it on fire. You will invoke the name of your god and I will invoke the name of God. The divinity that will respond by granting fire is God! All the people respond: - The proposal is good.

The priests of Baal prepare the altar with the quartered bullock. Then they invoke the name of Baal from morning until noon. They go around the altar, they jump, they shout at the top of their lungs: "Baal, answer us!" Answer us, Baal! But you don't hear a breath or an answer. They continue to jump more and more excited and shout louder and louder. Elijah, with arms crossed, makes fun of them and says: - Cry out louder, because he is a god! Maybe he's lost in thought, or he's busy in some business, or maybe he's on a journey ... If he's ever asleep, he'll wake up. Shout out, shout louder. But from Baal, there is no response, nor a sign of attention.

Elijah then commands all the people: - Come closer! And his voice resembles the hiss of a whip. Elijah builds the altar, digs around a small canal, and arranges the wood and the quartered bullock. Then he says: - Fill four jugs of water and pour them on the victim and on the wood. Do this three times. Water flows around the altar and even the Canaletto fills with water. Then Elijah, in a ringing voice, dresses her and her hair ruffled by the wind, says: - God, Lord, and God of Abraham, of Isaac and of Jacob! Today we know that you are the God of Israel and that I am your prophet! Answer me, Lord, and let the people know that you are the only true God! Convert, O Lord, their hearts! As soon as Elijah finishes this prayer, a globe of fire falls on the altar and consumes the victim and the wood and the stones in an instant and dries all the water of the canal. To this view all prostrate themselves with their faces to the ground and exclaim: - God is God! God is God!

Amos and Hosea

After the death of Elisha, God sends two other prophets to the northern kingdom to admonish the people and lead them back to the observance of the Law of Moses. The first of these prophets is Amos, a crude shepherd from Tekoa, whom God calls to his service with a voice similar to the roar of a lion. Amos lashes out, with an equally terrible voice, against the kings of Samaria and the corrupt court-goers. Driven out by order of King Jeroboam II, Amos returns to his flocks. But the first threat to the king and the people is the end of the kingdom and its leaders.

The second prophet who attempts the conversion of the northern kingdom is Hosea. He, unlike Amos, is the prophet of sweetness, of tenderness. God tries to take his people with good manners, using all his mercy. Hosea compares the people of Israel to a woman who has betrayed her husband. - God is the bridegroom of Israel - the prophet preaches -. God is willing to forgive his people, as a bridegroom who infinitely loves the bride is ready to welcome her into the house after it has been granted to lovers. But even the preaching of Hosea is useless. The people no longer hear words of threat, or expressions of tenderness. The northern kingdom, in 721 BC, was occupied by Sargon II, king of Assyria. The capital Samaria is devastated and almost all the inhabitants are deported. The kingdom of Ephraim is definitively erased from history and geography. The territory of the ten tribes of Israel is occupied by the Assyrians and becomes a colony of the empire.

The prophets of the kingdom of Judah

In the kingdom of Judah, or in the south, things do not go very differently. Even the kings of Judah are corrupt and depart from the Law of Moses. They honor the Canaanite gods and even go so far as to offer to those gods, false and cruel, human victims. Around the year 740 BC, God raises the greatest prophet of Israel: Isaiah in the southern kingdom. Isaiah's mission is to announce to God the punishment of God for the people's infidelities. For forty years Isaiah predicts misfortunes and punishments. But he too is unheard. Isaiah, however, does not limit himself to announcing catastrophes. He leaves hope open. After the terrible punishment that God prepares for his people, a remnant of Israel will survive and the kingdom of Judah will recover, according to the promise made by God to King David.

In the book of Isaiah the passion and death of the future Messiah are described in all details. It almost seems that the prophet contemplates Calvary and the cross where Jesus will be nailed. Even the prophet

Jeremiah, who begins to carry out his mission towards 620 BC, announces the end of the kingdom of Judah. Jeremiah does not threaten. He complains of the corruption of Jerusalem and contemplates the ruin of the city of David, the holy city, the city that God had chosen as his home. - Jerusalem has seriously sinned, - the prophet Jeremiah mourns - but God will punish his sins. Ah! How solitary the city once rich in people! It has become like a widow, the great one among the nations. Isaiah's threats and Jeremiah's lamentations are of no use. The corruption of the kingdom of Judah is total.

Other prophets also announce the imminent punishment. Israel has reached the bottom of the abyss along the slope. In the year 587 before Christ, the Babylonian king Nebuchadnezzar conquered the holy city with a powerful army. The siege lasts a long time. When hunger now dominates the city and there is no more bread for the population, a breach is opened in the walls. The Babylonian army enters Jerusalem, destroys the temple, throws it to the ground and shaves almost all the houses. The soldiers tear the bronze columns of the temple to pieces, destroy the Ark of the Covenant and steal all the sacred furnishings and vessels. Most of the population is deported to Babylon. The kingdom of Judah also disappears from history and geography. God's saving project seems to have failed miserably. A period of sorrow, but also reflection, begins for the chosen people. Israel slowly realizes that the catastrophe was caused by the unfaithfulness of the kings and the people.

During the exile of Babylon, other prophets lit the torch of hope. - It is not possible - pray the Israelites who kept themselves faithful to the Law of Moses - that you, O God, permanently abandon your people.

PART 2
THE PROPHETS OF EXILE - THE RETURN FROM EXILE - THE RESTORATION OF THE TEMPLE

The prophets of exile

And during the exile of Babylon, God who is faithful to the promises does not abandon his people. The punishment was necessary for Israel to become aware of its own infidelities and to return to its God. The prophet Ezekiel, who is also a priest, proclaims from the exile of Babylon that the temple of Jerusalem will be restored and that Israel will return home. Israel will rise again.

Now it's a pile of dry bones, but these bones will get covered in flesh and life will start again. Says Ezekiel: "Thus says the Lord: I will gather you among the nations and gather you from the lands where you have been scattered. I will give you the land of Israel again. I will take the heart of stone from your breast and I will give you a heart of flesh, so that you may follow my decrees and observe my laws. You will be my people again and I will be your God.

Even the prophet Jeremiah, who saw Jerusalem fall, foretells to the exiled people a new covenant between God and his people: - Thus says the Lord God: Behold, days will come in which with my people I will conclude a new alliance. Not like the covenant I made with their fathers when I took them by the hand to get them out of the land of Egypt: a covenant that they violated even though I was their Lord. This will be the covenant that I will conclude with my people: I will put my law in their minds; I will write it in their hearts. The hopes that the prophets Ezekiel and Jeremiah sow in the heart of the people of Israel exiled in Babylon do not only concern the return to their homeland and the restoration of the temple. These hopes go much further in time. They understand the definitive restoration and the new covenant that the Savior, the Messiah, the Son of God, Jesus of Nazareth will fulfil in the fullness of time.

The return from exile

Israel remains in exile in Babylon from 587 to 538 BC. During these fifty years, the chosen people never forget their distant homeland. Psalm 137, composed of an exile at that time, reveals the sentiments of Israel: On the rivers of Babylon, we sat there weeping at the memory of Zion. We hung our harps on the soil of that land. Those who had deported us asked us for words of the song. Songs of joy were asked of us by our oppressors: *"Sing to us the songs of*

Jerusalem!" How to sing the songs of the Lord in a foreign land? If I forget you, Jerusalem, let my right hand be paralyzed; stick your tongue to the palate, if I drop your memory, if I don't put Jerusalem above all my joy. In the year 538, the Persian emperor Cyrus, who had defeated the Babylonians, granted the exiled Jews in Babylon to return to Jerusalem. Cyrus gives back to the Jews the sacred objects removed from Nebuchadnezzar's army from the temple.

The emperor also agrees that having returned home, the Jews will rebuild the temple in Jerusalem. The first caravan of exiles marches towards the homeland led by Sesbassar. Other groups return to Jerusalem in random order. Certainly, the return to the Promised Land is not as glorious as the exiles had imagined. It is not the triumphal march of the times of Joshua. Indeed, the liberator is not even a son of Israel, but a pagan king: Cyrus. However, God maintained the promise made by the mouth of his prophets Isaiah, Jeremiah and Ezekiel. The salvation project painstakingly restarts. The time of the saviour is approaching.

The restoration of the temple

After returning to Palestine, the members of the small remnant of Israel, who took the name of Jews all belonging to the tribe of Judah, do not enjoy political autonomy. They are under Persian control. Indeed the land of Judah is a province of the empire of Cyrus and his successors. The Jews returned to their homeland face two major problems. On the one hand, they have to rebuild the temple of Jerusalem and much of the city. On the other hand, they must rediscover their roots, rebuild a culture, re-discover the identity lost as the people of God. At the first problem they put two fervent Jews: Ezra and Nehemiah.

In 515, twenty years after returning home, the temple is rebuilt. Instead, it is more difficult to find a lost identity. The post-exile prophets provide this task: Haggai, Zechariah, and Malachi. They try to rekindle faith in God and hope in the future Messiah in the hearts of the Jews. In 331 BC, Alexander the Great, the Macedonian, conquers Persia and, consequently, also Palestine. After the premature death of the great leader, the Macedonian empire is dismembered in two. First Palestine is disputed by the Egyptian kingdom of Alexandria, then by the Seleucids of Syria.

Now the kingdom of Judah will no longer be autonomous. All attempts by Jews against foreign invaders, such as those reported in the two Maccabees books, are suffocated in blood. In 63 BC, Pompey conquers Palestine and subjects it to the power of Rome. We are on the threshold of the New Testament.

PART I
JOB - DANIEL - TOBIAS

STORIES AND THE WISDOM OF ISRAEL (JOB -DANIEL -TOBIAS -ESTHER -JUDITH - WISDOM BOOKS)

PART 1
JOB - DANIEL - TOBIAS

The people of Israel, like so many other peoples have expressed throughout the centuries of its history literary works, stories, prayers, books of meditation and formation.

The Bible contains several essays on this cultural heritage of the chosen people.

The stories are not historical, but, taking their cue from real situations, they invent characters and events in order to instruct and build readers.

Job

"In the land of Uz there lived a man whose name was Job. This man was blameless and upright; he feared God and shunned evil. He had seven sons and three daughters, 3 and he owned seven thousand sheep, three thousand camels, five hundred yoke of oxen and five hundred donkeys, and had a large number of servants. He was the greatest man among all the people of the East."- Job 1:1-3

The book of Job attempts to give an answer to the question that man has always asked himself: Why do the just suffer? In the land of Uz lives a man called Job. He is whole and upright, fears God, and is alien to evil. He has seven sons and three daughters. He has seven thousand sheep, three thousand camels, five hundred pairs of oxen and five hundred donkeys. One day the Lord wants to test him. First, he takes away all his servants. Then, he makes his sons and daughters die. Finally, it strikes him with a serious and repulsive illness. But always the man of Uz welcomes the misfortunes saying: -

Nude I came out of my mother's breast and I will return you naked. The Lord has given, the Lord has taken away. Blessed be the name of the Lord.

Three friends come to see Job and begin to talk to him. Each of them tries to give an explanation to the sufferings of the right. Job, at the end, embittered by his misfortunes that cannot find human explanations, turns to God and asks him for an account of his work considered unjust. Then, God speaks to Job and tells him: -

Would you dare to judge me and do me wrong to be right? Am I not the one who governs the world with my wisdom? How can you understand the meaning of suffering?

Job then understands that pain, even if a man does not know how to explain it, has a value known only to God. Even Jesus will not explain the meaning of suffering but will accept it as a demonstration of love for the Father and for men. Only those who accept suffering can somehow understand it. At the end of the story, Job resigned and replied to God: - No one can understand the reasons why you act. But all you do is certainly for good. I knew you by hearsay, but now my eyes see you.

Daniel

"Among those who were chosen were some from Judah: Daniel, Hananiah, Mishael and Azariah. The chief official gave them new names: to Daniel, the name Belteshazzar; to Hananiah, Shadrach; to Mishael, Meshach; and to Azariah, Abednego. But Daniel resolved not to defile himself with the royal food and wine, and he asked the chief official for permission not to defile himself this way."- Daniel 1:6-8

The story of Daniel is set in Babylon during the exile of the Jews. The young Daniel is also among the deportees. He, with three other companions, is educated at the court of King Nebuchadnezzar. The four boys had to become pages, court servants. One day the king asks Daniel's friends to deny the God of Israel and to worship a golden statue. The three refuse. Then Nebuchadnezzar has them thrown into a fiery furnace. But young people rely on God and flames lick their bodies without burning them.

Daniel is also thrown into a pit of hungry lions, but the Lord saves him because the young man trusts him. The story of these boys thrown into the midst of dangers is the story of the good guys who have always been in contact with selfishness, violence and injustice. But God does not allow the wicked to prevail. In the end, the vouchers will win and the violent will be punished. In reality, those that seem strong are the real weak. One night Nebuchadnezzar makes a dream. He sees an enormous statue with a golden head, a chest and arms of silver, a belly and legs of bronze, and some feet of iron and partly of clay. While the king looks at the statue, a stone breaks away from the mountain, but not at the hands of a man, and goes to beat against the feet of the statue and shatters them. Then the iron, the bronze, the silver and the gold are also shattered and the whole statue is reduced to a handful of dust that the wind blows away. Daniel interprets Nebuchadnezzar's dream. - The statue - says the young man to the king - represents the powerful kingdoms of the earth founded on wealth, on strength. They are made of gold, silver, bronze, iron. They seem invincible, but they have feet of clay. The stone that is detached from the mountain represents the Lord. He will one day destroy the powerful and reduce them to dust.

Tobias

In the city of Nineveh lives a very good and charitable Jew named Tobi. He is blind and has a son named Tobias. In the distant city of Ecbatana lives a relative of his, Raguele, who has a daughter, Sara, very unhappy and unlucky. Tobi and Tobias are very poor. Tobi had lent money to a certain Gabriel who lives near Ecbatana but how to go there to collect the debt? Tobi is old and blind. Tobias is still a boy. And one day a young man shows up at the house of Tobit. He tells of being directed precisely towards Ecbatana and to know the streets well. Tobias trusts the young man and, with the blessing of his father, sets off with his travelling companion. Tobias's dog also follows them.

The journey is adventurous. Once Tobias is about to be eaten by a big fish. But the young man who accompanies him helps him to kill the animal, then advising him to preserve the gall. After other vicissitudes, the two young people arrive in Ecbatana. They collect the debt. Tobias meets Sara, falls in love with her and marries her. On his return, the fish's bile heals Tobi's blindness. When the time comes for Tobias to separate from the young stranger who was his guide, Tobi tells his son:

"We must pay for it." Let's give him half of the money we've collected.Tobias replies: - How can we reward him for everything he did? He freed me from the dangers, he recovered the money, he made me find a wife and, finally, he restored your sight to you.

Then the young stranger reveals himself: - I am Raphael - he says - an angel of God. HE himself sent me to you to help you. And after uttering these words, he disappears. The story teaches respect and love for parents. But above all, the story of Tobias shows the providence of God. He accompanies every man who entrusts himself to him on the roads of life. God wants to be close to the man to protect him and so that he can realize himself in total freedom.

PART 2
ESTHER - JUDITH - WISDOM IN ISRAEL

Esther

In Susa, a city of Persia lives a Jewish deportee named Mordecai. He discovered a conspiracy against the king of Persia, Ahasuerus. Mordecai has a very beautiful and very sweet niece named Ester. King Ahasuerus falls in love with her and marries her. But the ministers of Ahasuerus, who had been part of the plot against the king, hate so much Mordecai as Queen Esther. With deception, Haman, one of the king's ministers, obtained an edict from Ahasuerus with which he ordered the extermination of all the deported Jews. But Queen Esther, with her sweetness and humility, obtains the revocation of the edict from the king and thus saves her compatriots. The king then Haman hanged on the same post that the minister had prepared for Mordecai. The story teaches that sweetness and truth are always stronger than violence and deception.

Judith

Nebuchadnezzar, king of Babylon had waged war against Israel. The powerful Babylonian army, commanded by General Holoferne, besieged the

Jewish city of Betulia. The inhabitants of Betulia is now resigned to surrender. In the city lives a woman named Giuditta. She is young, fragile, poor, inexperienced in arms. Having heard that the city is about to surrender, Judith scolds her compatriots. Then he addresses this prayer to the Lord:

God, my God, listen to me. Our enemies are proud of their horses and riders; they boast of the strength of their infantrymen, they place their hope on shields and lances, on bows and slings. Instead, you are the God of the humble, you are the supporter of the derelicts, the refuge of the weak, the protector of the disheartened, and the saviour of the desperate. Give your people the proof that you are the Lord.

Having said this supplication, Judith rises from the ground, wears the most beautiful clothes she has and, together with her maid, introduces herself to the tent of Holofernes. The general was immediately struck by Giuditta's beauty and assigned her a private tent. After a few days Holofernes, with the imminent attack on Betulia, organized a sumptuous banquet for his commanders to which he also invited Judith. Holofernes drinks wine that night until they get drunk. When the captains' retreat into their tents, Giuditta grabs with two hands the sword of Holofernes asleep and, with all the strength of which he is capable, hits him several times on the neck until he cuts off his head. The death of the general disrupts the Babylonian army, which later, under the pressure of the inhabitants of Bethulia, is forced to flee. The Jews, on the work of a young, fragile, poor, inexperienced woman, are safe. The story shows that when the little ones, the weak, the poor when they rely on God, they always get the victory.

The wisdom in Israel

Numerous books of the Bible teach practical norms for an everyday living since wisdom was not so much an intellectual virtue, but a practical-moral one. The wise man, for the Jewish people, was the sage, he who knew how to behave on the most diverse occasions in life; he who knew the law of God and knew how to practice it, confirming his conduct to it, making his whole life uniform. The perfect sage then, besides knowing and practising the law of God, knew how to make it known to others, also inducing them to practice it. They are the sapiential books: the Proverbs, the Ecclesiastes, the Sirach, and the Wisdom.

According to these books, wisdom consists above all in fearing God and serving him in small daily actions. Among the sapiential books, the Psalms and the Song of Songs are of particular importance. The Canticle of Canticles exposes the love God has for man in a poetic form. This love is so sweet and so tender that it almost has the characteristics of love between two young spouses. But the comparison is only a pale image of how much God loves the man. God's love is infinitely sweeter and tenderer. The book of Psalms is a collection of prayers composed over many centuries. The Psalms are around 150 and were recited by the Jews in the various circumstances of life. Jesus himself recited the Psalms of the Old Testament very often. Therefore, till today the church uses these stupendous prayers during the worship that it renders to God.

NEW TESTAMENT
THE STORY OF JESUS
(MATTHEW'S GOSPELS
- MARK - LUKE - JOHN)

PART 1
THE WORD OF GOD - THE FOUR GOSPELS - THE BIRTH OF JESUS - JESUS PRESENTED AT THE TEMPLE - JESUS AMONG THE SAGES OF ISRAEL

The Word of God

"In the beginning was the Word, and the Word was with God, and the Word was God. The same was in the beginning with God. All things were made by him; and without him was not anything made that was made. In him was life; and the life was the light of men. And the light shineth in darkness; and the darkness comprehended it not."- John 1:1-5

With the Word, God first creates heaven and earth. With the Word, he calls Abraham and elects him progenitor of the chosen people. The same Word God addresses to Moses to indicate to him the mission he must fulfil. The word of God is also that of the prophets of Israel, addressed to the people to convert and return to the observance of the law. Despite all these interventions of the Word, humanity is still far from its Creator. The sin of the first men continues to produce egoism, violence, injustice, deceit, death in the world. Then God decides a radical and definitive intervention. The Word becomes flesh, it becomes a man.

Jesus of Nazareth, descendant according to the blood of the lineage of David, is the Word of God, generated by the Father, equal to the Father, God as the Father and as the Holy Spirit. Jesus is a true man and true God, Son of Mary and Son of God. God's plan foresees the salvation of humanity, the happiness of men. Man does not have the possibility to save himself. Jesus, the Word of the Father, brings to earth the happy news that the Father loves every man and is willing to forgive every sin provided that man is converted. Jesus, Word of the Father, promises a life beyond death, a life of happiness next to the Father. Jesus reveals to the men the project of the Father and, at the same time, he realizes what he says. Jesus loves every man, especially if he is weak, small, poor, helpless, mild, and suffering.

Jesus forgives the sins of the men who come to him repenting. Jesus, with his resurrection, guarantees us that there is a happy life after death. Jesus assures every man who believes in him that salvation is possible because he himself has realized it. Jesus is a new Law because every man, to be saved, must welcome him, serve him and imitate him. Jesus is the new Covenant because it establishes a relationship of love between God and man. Jesus is a Prophet because he speaks in the name of the Father.

He is King because to him the Father has entrusted all men. Jesus is the Anointed of the Father, he is the Christ. Jesus is a Priest because he offers the Father himself, in total obedience, to redeem the world. After many failed attempts, the project of salvation with Jesus is fully realized. After Jesus, every man can be saved if he accepts the forgiveness of the Father if he experiences the love of the Father, If, in turn, he loves and forgives his brothers. The fullness of time has come. Humanity is ready to receive the message of Jesus. In the time of Herod the Great, king of Judea, while the emperor Caesar Augustus rules in Rome, the Word of God becomes flesh in the womb of the Virgin Mary and lives in the midst of us.

Palestine at the time of Jesus

In the year 40 BC, Palestine, submitted to the Roman governor of the province of Syria, was entrusted to Herod the Great, a friend and ally of the Romans, an ambitious and cruel man. Herod is a Jew with ancestors of foreign origin. Also, for this reason, he is hated by his countrymen. Herod dies shortly after the birth of Jesus. After his death, the kingdom of Palestine is divided between three of his sons.

Archelaus is named head of the people of Judea and Samaria, south of Palestine. Filippo is appointed the head of the territory east of the Jordan (Transjordan). Herod Antipas becomes head of the Galilee, the most northern region of Palestine. After the death of Archelaus, which occurred in the year 6 after Christ, the territory of Judea and Samaria is ruled by procurators of Roman origin. Pontius Pilate rules the territory from 26 to 36 after Christ.

The four Gospels

The story of Jesus is told in the first four books of the New Testament called the Gospels. The term gospel means *"good news"*. The Gospels, in fact, announce the news of the salvation of humanity carried out by Jesus. The gospels were written from about 60 to 90 After Christ. The evangelists - Matthew, Mark, Luke and John - collected the story of Jesus as it was preached by the apostles. Matthew and John are themselves apostles of Jesus. Mark reports the preaching of Peter and Luke is a disciple of the apostle Paul. Matthew presents Jesus as the Messiah of Israel, the son of David. The Gospel of Matthew announces the kingdom of God established by Jesus. Mark presents Jesus as the Son of God and, at the same time, as the Son of man. The Gospel of Luke proposes Jesus as the saviour of all humanity. The Gospel of John, written last, presents Jesus as the Word of the Father, anointed of God (= Christ) and develops the theme of God's love for man.

Jesus' childhood stories are reported only in the gospels of Matthew and Luke. The stories, while preserving their historicity, contain many details imagined by the authors for an edifying purpose. The birth of Jesus recalls the births described in the Old Testament. Other episodes of Jesus 'childhood is also related to facts and characters from the Old Testament.

The birth of Jesus

"In the sixth month of Elizabeth's pregnancy, God sent the angel Gabriel to Nazareth, a town in Galilee, to a virgin pledged to be married to a man named Joseph, a descendant of David. The virgin's name was Mary. The angel went to her and said, "Greetings, you who are highly favored! The Lord is with you." Mary was greatly troubled at his words and wondered what kind of greeting this might be. 30 But the angel said to her, "Do not be afraid, Mary; you have found favor with God. You will conceive and give birth to a son, and you are to call him Jesus. ""- Luke 1:26-31

Jesus was born in Bethlehem of Judea in the time of King Herod the Great. The mother of Jesus is Mary of Nazareth, the betrothed of Joseph. Mary is a poor girl, but rich in faith. God entrusts to her the mission of giving the Savior to the world. Mary accepts God's proposal and Jesus incarnate in her womb through the work of the Holy Spirit. Joseph, because he is a just man when he realizes that his betrothed is pregnant decides to leave her in secret. Warned in a dream by the voice of God, he accepts the mystery of that miraculous conception and agrees to marry Mary. The time comes for Mary to give birth. Just in those days a decree of Caesar Augustus orders the census of the entire population of Palestine. Each head of the family must go to their home city.

Joseph is a native of Bethlehem in Judea, the same city where King David was born. Thus Joseph and Mary descend from Nazareth to the south and arrive in Bethlehem. Now, while they are in that place, Maria gives birth to the child, wraps him in swaddling clothes and places him in a manger because the young spouses had not found a place in the hotel.

Some shepherds watched their flocks nearby rush to worship the baby. The child is called Jesus. A few days later, they come to the place where the child was born, some astrologers or magi to worship him. They represent all the pagans. By welcoming Jesus, the three wise men attest that salvation is open to all peoples.

Jesus presented to the temple

"When the time came for the purification rites required by the Law of Moses, Joseph and Mary took him to Jerusalem to present him to the Lord (as it is written in the Law of the Lord, "Every firstborn male is to be consecrated to the Lord"), and to offer a sacrifice in keeping with what is said in the Law of the Lord: 'a pair of doves or two young pigeons.'"- Luke 2:22-24

When the child turns forty days, Mary and Joseph present him at the temple of Jerusalem as prescribed in the Law of Moses: Every firstborn male should be consecrated to the Lord. In the temple, there is an old priest named Simeon. He takes the child in his arms and thanks to God for giving him the consolation of seeing the Savior before closing his eyes forever. To Mary, the priest foretells many sufferings: - *This child is a sign of contradiction* - says Simeon in a trembling voice

- Few will accept Him, many will reject Him. And you, Maria, will have to suffer for this child. You will have as a sword planted in the heart.

Simeon, who welcomes Jesus in his arms, represents all the people of Israel who had been waiting for the Messiah for so many centuries and now, finally, he sees the promises made by God realized.

Jesus among the sages of Israel

Joseph, Mary and Jesus return to Nazareth after the death of Herod the Great. Jesus grows and becomes stronger. He is a boy full of wisdom because God's grace is above him. When Jesus turns twelve he goes with Mary and Joseph on a pilgrimage to Jerusalem, the holy city. Every year the Jews used to go to the temple during the holidays, like the Passover celebration that reminds of Israel's exit from the slavery of Egypt.

When Mary and Joseph go back into the caravan to return to Nazareth they realize that Jesus is not with them. After three days of frantic research, they finally find him in the temple. Jesus is in the midst of the sages of Israel. There are the scribes, who practice the profession of transcribing and interpreting the sacred writings. There are Pharisees, who consider themselves scrupulous observers of the Law of Moses. There are the Sadducees, aristocrats, conservatives and sympathizers of the Roman rulers. And finally, there are the priests, the men of worship, dedicated to the service of the temple. Jesus is in their midst. He questions them and speaks of the new kingdom, founded on love, which the Father wants to establish among men.

The wise men of Israel admired the intelligence and wisdom of the boy. Even Mary and Joseph in that circumstance remain amazed. They still do not fully understand the mission that God has entrusted to them: to guard and educate the Savior of the world. Jesus returns with Mary and Joseph to Nazareth and is obedient to them. And his mother kept all these things inside her heart.

PART 2
JOHN ANNOUNCES THE SAVIOR - JESUS ANNOUNCES THE KINGDOM - THE DISCIPLES OF JESUS - THE WORDS OF JESUS

John announces the Savior

"The people were waiting expectantly and were all wondering in their hearts if John might possibly be the Messiah. John answered them all, "I baptize you with water. But one who is more powerful than I will come, the straps of whose sandals I am not worthy to untie. He will baptize you with the Holy Spirit and fire. His winnowing fork is in his hand to clear his threshing floor and to gather the wheat into his barn, but he will burn up the chaff with unquenchable fire.'"- Luke 3:15-17

John, son of Elizabeth, a relative of Mary, is about the same age as Jesus. When Jesus turns thirty, John begins to preach the conversion of sins among the people. He wears rough robes and rails against the corruption of King Herod Antipas. And his voice resembles the mighty voice of the ancient prophets of Israel. John cries to the people:

"Get converted from your sins!" divide the goods among you, help the poorest, and do not abuse the weak.

John brings men and women down to the Jordan River and pours water on their heads, a symbol of purification. Many Israelites are convinced that John is the Messiah. But he says: - No, I am not the Messiah. I baptize you with water. But someone stronger than me will come, to whom I am not worthy to untie the rope of his sandals. He will take away all the sins of the world. With other exhortations, John announces the good news to the people. Jesus leaves the house of Nazareth and, after having spent a long period of prayer in the desert; he goes to the Jordan and is baptized by John. From that moment his public mission began. Sometime later, Herod Antipas, blamed by Giovanni for all the wickedness he committed, had him imprisoned and then beheaded. Thus the last prophet of Israel and the first announcer of the good news died.

Jesus announces the kingdom

Jesus begins his mission in Galilee, where he grew up. In Nazareth, one day on Saturday, Jesus went to the synagogue to read and comment on the Word of God written in the scrolls. The scroll of the prophet Isaiah is given to him by the attendants of the synagogue. Jesus opens the scroll and reads this passage: -

The Spirit of God is upon me. He anointed me with anointing and sent me to announce a happy message to the poor, to proclaim liberty to the prisoners and sight to the blind, and to release the oppressed and to heal those whose hearts are broken.

Then, Jesus calmly rolls up the scroll, hands it to the attendant and sits down. Everyone's eyes in the synagogue are fixed on him. Jesus has a deep and mysterious look. His long hair frames his majestic and, at the same time, very loving face. Jesus has a warm and fascinating voice. Sometimes, the voice takes on tender and very sweet tones; sometimes it is severe and lashing. He wears a seamless tunic, woven in one piece from top to bottom. The tunic comes to cover his feet. Jesus, in turn, fixes all those present. Then chanting the words he says: - Today this writing has been fulfilled that you have heard with your ears. Today, the Messiah of God is among you. All look at each other and ask themselves d: - How can this man claim to be the Messiah, the Lord's Anointed, the Savior announced by the prophet Isaiah? Is he not Joseph's son, - the carpenter? And doesn't his mother live among us? Jesus stands up and dominates the whole assembly with his tall stature. He repeats: - *Today the kingdom of which the prophet Isaiah speaks has begun among you. But you don't believe me. No prophet is welcome at home.* Then, all in the synagogue stand up full of disdain. They take Jesus and push him out. Then, they lead him to the edge of the mountain on which their city is situated to throw him down the precipice. But Jesus, going through them, goes away. From the beginning of his mission, Jesus understands that his people do not intend to welcome him. The world does not recognize it. Jesus came among his people, but his own did not accept it. Once again Israel refuses the salvation that God, in his infinite mercy, intends to propose to them..

The disciples of Jesus

Jesus shows with the works that the kingdom of God is present in the world. Jesus walks the streets of Galilee and heals the sick affected by all kinds of evil. A crowd begins to follow him. Everyone wants to hold him, but Jesus does not stop in any city. He repeats with his eyes turned towards the sky: - *I must announce the kingdom of God in all cities. This is why I was sent*.

One day Jesus is near the Sea ofGalilee or Lake Tiberias. The crowd gathers around him to hear his word. Jesus sees two boats moored to the shore. The fishermen have come down and wash the nets. Jesus goes up on a boat, which was of Simon Peter, and begs him to move away from the ground a little. Then, he sits and teaches the crowd from the boat. When he has finished speaking, he says to Simone:

"Take off and drop the fishing nets." Simone says: - "Teacher, we have struggled all night and we have not taken anything, but on your word, I will throw the nets".

Simone and the other fishermen who are in the boat throw their nets and take an enormous amount of fish. The nets almost break. Then they mention the companions of the other boat who come to help them. They come and fill both boats with fish to the point that they almost sink.

In noticing this miracle, Simon Peter throws himself at Jesus' knees and says: - *"Lord, get away from me because I am a sinner"*. Even James and John, sons of Zebedee and associates of Simon, are taken by great astonishment. Jesus says to Simon, to James and to John: - ***"Do not be afraid. From now on, you will be fishers of men"***. And those, throw the boats on the ground, leave everything and follow him.

Peter, James and John are the first three disciples of Jesus. Others then follow him: Andrew, Philip, Bartholomew, Matthew, Thomas, James son of Alphaeus, Simon nicknamed Zealot, Judas Thaddeus and Judas Iscariot. The disciples of Jesus, or apostles, are altogether twelve, like the twelve tribes of Israel.

The words of Jesus

With his twelve friends, Jesus walks the streets of Galilee teaching the crowds. It doesn't have a house; it doesn't even have a stone to lay its head on. Jesus speaks in a new way, with simplicity and firmness. He says things that were never heard before. He declares that the poor are blessed, that the myths will inherit the earth, that the hunger for justice will be satisfied. He rails against the rich who have closed their hearts to God and to their brothers. - *"Love your enemies"* - preach Jesus – *"and do well to those who hate you"*.

"Bless those who curse you, and pray for those who mistreat you. To those who hit you on the cheek, you also offer the other. Be merciful, as your Father is merciful. Do not judge and you will not be judged Forgive and you will be forgiven. Give and it will be given to you. Do not do good works to be admired by men. You cannot serve God and money. Don't worry about what you will eat or how you will dress. Your heavenly Father will think of you. Seek first the kingdom of God and his justice. How much you want men to do to you, you also do it to them". The crowds are astonished at the words of Jesus.

He teaches as one who has authority and not like their scribes. The words of Jesus irritate the powerful and the violent, while they console the poor and the myths. Jesus also speaks in parables. The parable is a story, a simile that refers to concrete facts of life. Jesus says that the kingdom of God is like a pearl that a man finds in a field. The man sells everything to buy that field and possess the pearl. Jesus says that we must love our neighbour in a concrete way and not just in words. And He tells of a Samaritan who meets a wounded man on the street and cares for him paying in person. Jesus says that the heavenly Father loves every sinner who returns to his home after having squandered all wealth in illicit pleasures. The crowds listen to Jesus' words full of wonder. Everyone realizes that that man with a deep and mysterious look is really a great prophet, an envoy of the Lord.

PART 3

YOU ARE THE SON OF GOD - JESUS ENTERS JERUSALEM - THE LAST SUPPER - JESUS FORETELLS PETER'S DENIAL

You are the Son of God

Jesus performs numerous miracles according to what was written in the scroll of the prophet Isaiah. The kingdom of God has really begun because Jesus gives back sight to the blind and hearing to the deaf. Jesus multiplies the bread to feed the crowds that follow him. Heal the lepers, makes the lame walk and above all heals the hearts of repentant sinners. Jesus shows Himself Lord of living and death. Set a storm in the Sea of Galilee and raise a girl near Capernaum and a young man in the city of Nain.

The scribes, the Pharisees, the priests of the temple are irritated by the words and miracles of Jesus. They think that he wants to abolish the Law of Moses. They feel touched by the accusations that Jesus addresses to the selfish, the hypocrites, and the rich with a hard heart. - But who is this Jesus of Nazareth? - They wonder worried. The same question, one day, Jesus addresses his disciples in the city of Caesarea

Philippi: "Who says the people that I am"? - Jesus asks. The answer: - John the Baptist, others say that you are Elias and others that you are Jeremiah or one of the prophets. Jesus tells them: - "And who do you say that I am"? Simon Peter answers: -

"You are the Christ, the Son of the living God". And Jesus: - "Blessed are you, Simon son of John, because neither flesh nor blood revealed it to you, but my Father who is in heaven. And I say to you: You are Peter and on this rock, I will build my church that no power can ever destroy".

From that day Jesus begins to openly tell his disciples that he must go to Jerusalem and that he must suffer much because of the scribes, Pharisees and priests of the temple and be killed and resurrected on the third day.

Jesus enters Jerusalem- Matthew 21:1-11, Mark 11:1-11, Luke 19:28-44, and John 12:12-19

Jesus leaves Galilee and goes down, with his apostles, along the roads of Samaria and Judea. When they are close to Jerusalem, Jesus sends two apostles to take a donkey. Jesus ascends the donkey and enters the city. The crowd that always followed Jesus and the inhabitants of the holy city give him great honours. People shake palm branches and spread their cloaks along the way. Everyone, especially children, shouts - Hosanna to the son of David!

Blessed is he who comes in the name of the Lord. Jesus smiles, but there is a shadow of sadness in his deep and mysterious eyes.

The scribes, the Pharisees and the priests of the temple are in agitation. They still ask themselves: "Well, who is he?" Jesus enters the temple of Jerusalem and drives out all those he finds there to buy and sell. He turns over the tables of the money changers and the chairs of the sellers of doves and tells them: - God's house is a house of prayer, but you make it a den of thieves. And the voice of Jesus resembles the hiss of a whip.

Last dinner- Mt. 26:17–30, Mk. 14:12–26, Lk. 22:7–39 and Jn. 13:1–17:26

The priests of the temple are furious against Jesus. They try in every way to take it to stand trial. But they fear the crowd and are undecided about what to do. Then one of the twelve apostles, Judas Iscariot, presents himself before the priests and says: - "How much do you want to give me to give Him to you"? Those set him thirty silver coins. From that moment, Judah seeks a favourable opportunity to deliver Jesus to the priests of the temple.

In those days the Jews celebrate the feast of Easter to commemorate Israel's exit from the slavery of Egypt. Jesus also wishes to make Easter with his disciples. On Thursday evening, Jesus goes to the table with the twelve. While eating, Jesus says: -I have ardently desired to eat with you this Easter before my passion. Then Jesus takes a slice of bread, blesses it, breaks it and distributes it to the apostles saying: - Take and eat. This is my body that is given to you. Do this in memory of me. In the same way, after having dinner, he takes a glass of wine and says: - This cup is the new covenant in my blood that is poured for you. With these words and these gestures, Jesus, during the last supper, institutes the Eucharist. Bread and wine become his body and his blood. Jesus thus maintains the promise that one day he made to the apostles: -

My Father will give you the bread that comes from heaven, the real one. I am the bread of life.

Your fathers ate the desert manna and died. I am the living bread that came down from heaven. If one eats of this bread he will live forever and the bread that I will give is my flesh for the life of the world. After establishing the Eucharist, Jesus says: "Truly, truly, I say to you, one of you will betray me". And the voice of Jesus is imbued with a sense of infinite sadness.

The apostles look at one another. They don't know who Jesus is talking about. John, the apostle whom Jesus loved more than any other, lays his head on Jesus' chest and asks him in a whisper: *"Lord, who is he?"* Jesus replies: - *"He is the one for whom I will dip a morsel and give it to him"*. And dipping a morsel of bread on the plate, he hands it to Judas Iscariot, saying: - *"What you have to do, do it as soon as possible"*. None of the apostles understands Jesus' words. Judas, keeping his eyes down, takes the morsel and immediately leaves the room. Outside its night now.

Jesus foretells Peter's denial

"About an hour later another asserted, "Certainly this fellow was with him, for he is a Galilean." Peter replied, "Man, I don't know what you're talking about!" Just as he was speaking, the rooster crowed. The Lord turned and looked straight at Peter. Then Peter remembered the word the Lord had spoken to him: "Before the rooster crows today, you will disown me three times." And he went outside and wept bitterly."- Luke 22:59-62

After Judas Iscariot came out, Jesus said to the eleven: "Children, I am still with you for a little while. I give you a new commandment: love one another as I have loved you. From this, they will know that you are my disciples". Simone Peter asks"Lord, where are you going"? Jesus replies: "Where I go for now you cannot follow me. You will follow me later". Peter, with a firm voice and leaning forward the broad chest, replies: "Why can't I follow you? I will give my life for you!" And Jesus: - "Will you give my life for me? Verily, verily, I say unto you, before the cock crows in the morning, thou shalt have denied me three times". And the voice of Jesus is imbued with a hint of infinite sadness. Then he continues: - "I'm going to prepare you a place and the place where I'm going you know the way". Thomas says: "We don't know where you are going." How can we know the way? Jesus replies: - "I am the way, the truth and the life. Those who know me also know the Father". Philip says: "Lord, show us the Father and that's enough". Jesus answers: -"For three years have I been with you and you have not known me, Phillips?" Whoever saw me saw the Father and while Jesus speaks these words his eyes are even more profound and mysterious.

PART 4
THE PRAYER OF JESUS - IN THE GARDEN OF GETHSEMANE - ARREST OF JESUS AND DENIAL OF PETER - JESUS IS CONDEMNED TO DEATH

The prayer of Jesus

Then, raising your eyes to heaven, Jesus says:
- Father, the time has come. Glorify your Son, so that the Son may glorify you. Because you gave him power over every human being, so that he may give eternal life to all those you gave him. This is eternal life: that they know you, the only true God, and the one you sent, Jesus Christ. I made your name known to the men you gave me. They were yours and you gave them to me. The words you gave to me I gave them to them. Your word is the truth. I do not pray only for these, but also for those who by their word will believe in me; because all are one, like you and me, Father, we are one. Father, I want those who gave me may one day contemplate my glory. You loved me before the creation of the world, the love with which you loved me both in them and I in them.

In the Garden of Gethsemane

Jesus leaves the hall with his eleven apostles and sets out towards a farm nearby called Gethsemane. They stop under some olive trees. Jesus tells the apostles: *"Sit here while I pray."* Then he takes with him Peter, James and John and with them, he takes a few steps away. He tells them: - *My soul is sad to death. Stay here and watch.* Going on as a stone's throw, Jesus throws himself on the ground and says: - *My father! Remove this cup from me. But not what I want to accomplish, but what you want.* Back, he finds the three favourite apostles asleep. He shakes Peter and tells him: - *Simone, are you asleep? Weren't you able to watch an hour alone?* Three times Jesus goes away and three times, returning, he finds the apostles asleep. Jesus is alone on that night. His closest friends are indifferent to his anguish.

The arrest of Jesus and denial of Peter

And immediately Judas Iscariot arrives and with him a crowd with swords and sticks sent by the high priests, the scribes and the Pharisees. Judas approaches Jesus, throws his arms around his neck and tells him: - Master. Then he kisses him, a slimy kiss like a snake. It is the agreed signal. – Who I will kiss, is Jesus. Stop it! - Judas had told the crowd. They put their hands on Jesus and arrest him. All the apostles flee in fear and abandon their friend and teacher. Jesus is led by the high priest Caiaphas to be interrogated. Peter follows Jesus from afar and enters

203

the courtyard of the palace of Caiaphas. The concierge asks her: - *Perhaps you are also this man's disciples?* Peter replies: - *I am not.*

While Caiaphas questions Jesus, Peter warms up next to a fire lit in the courtyard. They ask him for the second time: - *Are you one of his disciples?* Peter denies saying: - *I have never seen that man.* The rooster sings and Peter recalls the words of Jesus: Before the cock crows you will have denied me three times. Comes out of the courtyard and cries bitterly. Even Judas Iscariot regrets having betrayed the master. But, unlike Peter, his heart is too proud to cry. That same night he throws the thirty silver coins into the temple then move away and hang himself from a tree.

Jesus is condemned to death

The priests of the temple cannot condemn to death because the Roman procurator Pontius Pilate commands in Judea. He alone has the power of life and death over the Jews. Therefore the priests have Jesus led by Pilate. In front of the prosecutor the priests falsely accuse Jesus: - We found him who incited the people and prevented people from paying taxes to Caesar. He also claims to be the king of the Jews. Pilate asks Jesus: - *Are you the king of the Jews?* Jesus replies: - *You say so.* Pilate shrugs his shoulders and tells the priests and the gathered crowd: *"I find no fault in this man."* But they insist: *"If he wasn't a criminal, we wouldn't have handed him over."* Pilate then sends Jesus to King Herod Antipas, but even Herod cannot condemn Jesus. Jesus is led back by Pilate. The prosecutor again tries to save Jesus. He questions him: *"So you are king?"* And Jesus answers for the second time: - *You say it: I am king. But my kingdom is not here below. I came into the world to bear witness to the truth. Anyone on the side of truth, listen to my voice.* Pilate is impatient. Sighing deeply, he says, *"What is the truth?"* Pilate does not wait for the answer. He proposes to the crowd to exchange the life of Jesus with that of a true criminal, Barabbas. But the crowd, stirred up by the priests, shouts: - *Crucify Jesus; otherwise you are not a friend of Caesar.* Pilate, seeing that the tumult grows, he washes his hands in front of the crowd and says resigned: - *I am not responsible for the blood of this man.* See you. Then he leaves Barabbas free and, after having Jesus scourged, gives him to the soldiers to be crucified.

PART 5
JESUS ASCENDS CALVARY - CRUCIFIXION AND DEATH OF JESUS - JESUS RISES AGAIN - JESUS APPEARS TO THE APOSTLES

Jesus ascends Calvary

The soldiers weave a crown of thorns; place it on Jesus' head, then put a reed in his right hand. They kneel before him and mock him: *"Hail, king of the Jews!"* And spitting on him, they take the reed from him and strike him on the head. Then, they tie a horizontal pole to his shoulders and lead him out to Mount Calvary to crucify him. While Jesus climbs Calvary, the soldiers take a certain Simon of Cyrene and put the cross on him for him because Jesus is no longer able to carry him. A crowd of people and women follows Jesus. The women, among whom there is also the mother of Jesus, cry and beat their chests. Jesus comforts her saying: - *Daughters of Jerusalem, do not weep over me, but rather weep over yourself and your children.* With this expression, Jesus means that he dies innocent because of the sins of men. Together with Jesus, two criminals are also led to being executed.

Crucifixion and death of Jesus

When they reach the place of crucifixion, the soldiers take away from Jesus the seamless tunic, woven in one piece from top to bottom. Then they nail Jesus' wrists to the horizontal pole. Then they raise the pole on the vertical one already planted on the ground. Finally, on the vertical pole, they nail the feet of Jesus. With Jesus, the soldiers also crucify the two criminals, one on the right and one on the left. Jesus says: - *Father, forgive them because they do not know what they are doing. The people are going to see.* Instead, the priests of the temple, the scribes and the Pharisees mocked Jesus saying: - *He saved the others. Save yourself, if it is the Christ of God, his chosen one.* One of the evildoers also taunts Jesus. The other man prays: - *Jesus, remember me when you enter your kingdom.* Jesus answers him: *"Truly I tell you; today you will be with me in paradise.*

Under the cross of Jesus are his mother and John, the apostle whom Jesus loved. Seeing her mother, Jesus says in a sweet voice: *"Woman here is your son."* Then he says to the disciple: *"Here is your mother."* Jesus prays to the Father reciting *Psalm 22* which begins with this invocation: - *My God, my God, why have you forsaken me?* Then the psalm goes on: - *From me, O God, do not stay away because anguish is near and nobody helps me.* From noon until three in the afternoon Jesus agonizes and prays on the cross.

Around three in the afternoon Jesus, shouting with a loud voice, says: - *Father, in your hands I commit my spirit.* And having said that, he puts his head on his shoulder and dies.

Jesus dies on the eve of the Passover. The next day, Saturday is a solemn feast. It is not tolerable that the bodies of the crucifixes remain hung on the crosses. The priests, therefore, asked Pilate that the bodies be removed. Pilate agrees. So the soldiers come and break the legs of the two crucified criminals to hasten their death. The soldiers, seeing that Jesus is already dead, do not break his legs, but one of them strikes him in the side with a spear and immediately the last blood mixed with serum comes out of the wound. A certain Joseph d'Arimatea and a certain Nicodemus collect the body of Jesus and, with some women, wrap it in bandages together with aromatic oils. Nearby there is a garden and in the garden a new sepulchre carved into the rock, in which no one had yet been laid. There they lay Jesus. Then, they close the tomb with a heavy boulder.

Jesus rises again

After Saturday, some women go early to the tomb of Jesus. Women carry aromatic oils. On the day of the deposition from the cross, Jesus' body was arranged quickly for burial. Now the women intend to complete the work. Along the way the women say to each other: - Who will roll the boulder from the entrance to the tomb? But when they reached the place, they saw that the boulder had already rolled away, although it was very heavy. The women enter the tomb and see a young man, sitting on the right, dressed in a white robe. Women are afraid. But the young man, smiling, tells them: -

Don't be afraid! You seek Jesus of Nazareth, the crucifix. It has risen. It is not here. Now go, tell his disciples and Peter that he precedes you in Galilee.

Jesus appears to the apostles

On the evening of that same day, the first after Saturday, Jesus appears to his disciples in the cenacle room for fear of the Jews. Jesus stops among them and says: - *Peace be with you.* Then Jesus shows them his hands and his side. And the disciples rejoice to see the Lord. Eight days later Jesus appears again to the disciples. To Thomas Jesus, he makes the wounds of his hands and his sides touch with his finger.

Jesus appears numerous times to his apostles until they are convinced that he has truly risen from the dead. Now, the apostles must become witnesses of Jesus' resurrection. They will have to announce to all men that Jesus has conquered death. This is happy news. Jesus, rising from the dead, defeated the last enemy of man. Jesus erased sin from the world and subjected death, a consequence of sin. After Jesus, men can, in turn, overcome sin. They can overcome the fear of death because Jesus, with his resurrection, ignited in men the certain hope of eternal life. Many other signs Jesus does after his resurrection in the presence of his disciples, but they were not written in this book. These have been written, because you believe that Jesus is the Christ, the Son of God and because, believing, you have life in his name.

THE HISTORY OF THE CHURCH (ACTS OF THE APOSTLES - APOSTOLIC LETTERS - APOCALYPSE)

PART 1
JESUS ESTABLISHES THE CHURCH - JESUS RETURNS TO THE FATHER - THE FIRST CHRISTIAN COMMUNITY

Jesus establishes the church

After the resurrection, Jesus manifests himself one day to the disciples at the Sea of Galilee or Lake of Tiberias. Together we find Simon Peter, the sons of Zebedee and others. They go fishing and when they return to the ground they see a fire of embers. Next, to the fire there is a man. The man says: - *Bring some of the fish you took*. And his voice is firm and sweet. None of the disciples dares ask the man: *"Who are you?"* Everyone knows well that it is the Lord. When Jesus and the disciples finished eating the fish cooked on the grill, Jesus said to Simon Peter: - *Simon, son of John, do you love me more than these?* He replies: - *Of course, Lord, you know that I love you.* He tells him: - *Feed my lambs.*

He asks him for the second time: - Simon, do you love me? He replies: "Of course, Lord, you know it." He tells him: - Feed my sheep. He asks him for the third time: - Simon, do you love me? He replies: -

Lord, you know everything; you know that I love you. He tells him: - Feed my sheep.

Jesus, asking these three questions to Peter, wants to remind him of the triple denial that took place in the courtyard of Caiaphas. To feed the sheep of Jesus, that is, to become the head of the church, the pastor of the new people of God, above all love is necessary. In the church, authority is a service of love for the brothers. Peter, who recognizes that he is fragile, can better understand, and therefore love, those who are weak, small, sinners in the church.

Jesus returns to the Father

The eleven go to Galilee on the mountain that Jesus had fixed to them. It is the last meeting that the apostles have with their teacher. Jesus says: -

Go and teach all nations, baptizing them in the name of the Father, the Son and the Holy Spirit. Teach them to observe all that I have commanded you. Behold, I am with you every day, until the end of the world.

Then he leads them to Bethany and, raising his hands, blesses them. As he blesses them, he detaches himself from them and rises to the sky. And they, after having worshipped him, return to Jerusalem in Judea. In the heart of the eleven, there is so much melancholy and so much nostalgia for the sky. Jesus' mission is accomplished. Now, the salvation realized by Jesus must be made known throughout the world. The book

213

of the Acts of the Apostles, written by Luke, narrates the spread of the gospel during the early times after Jesus returned to the right hand of the Father. The descent of the Holy Spirit the apostles, having returned to Jerusalem, elect Matthias in place of Judas Iscariot, the traitor. The apostles live together in the hall where Jesus had established the Eucharist. They are assiduous and agree in prayer together with some women and with Mary, the mother of Jesus. Fifty days have now passed since the resurrection of Jesus. It is Pentecost day. The Jews celebrate the feast of renewal of the covenant with God. As the day is coming to an end the apostles are all together in the same place. Suddenly a roar comes from the sky, like a wind that beats down vigorously, and fills the whole house. Tongues appear as of fire that divides and rests on each of them. And the apostles are full of the Holy Spirit and begin to speak in other languages, as the Spirit gives them the power to express themselves. The Holy Spirit, promised by Jesus to the apostles, is the love that the Father has for the Son and the Son has for the Father. It is also the love that God has for men, an infinite, perfect, concrete love, that is not a simple feeling, but a Person, the third Person of the Most Holy Trinity. The Holy Spirit strengthens the will, warms the heart, illuminates the mind, unites the church, consoles and sanctifies. The Holy Spirit reminds men of all that Jesus said and helps them to realize it. From the day of Pentecost the apostles, strengthened in faith, with firmness and enthusiasm, begin the preaching of the gospel according to the command of Jesus. They announce the good news of salvation to the ends of the earth.

The first Christian community

Hearing the roar like wind blowing down, a crowd gathers in front of the cenacle. The apostles open the doors of the house and go out into the street. Peter addresses these words to the crowd in Jerusalem: - Men of Judea and all of you who are in Jerusalem. God raised Jesus Christ from the dead and we are all witnesses. Now Jesus is at the right hand of the Father in Heaven. The Holy Spirit whom he had promised, he poured over us, as you can see and hear. Know, therefore, all Israel that God has made Jesus, that you have crucified him, as Lord. Some Jews mock the apostles and say: - *They got drunk on must.* Many, on the other hand, feel pierced by the words of Peter and ask: - *What should we do?* Peter replies: -

Repent of your sins and let each of you be baptized in the name of Jesus. Afterwards, you will receive the gift of the Holy Spirit.

Many Jews become Christians that day. They are together; they put their goods in common, celebrate the Eucharist and praise God.

215

PART 2
THE FIRST PERSECUTIONS - THE FIRST MARTYR OF THE CHURCH - THE CONVERSION OF SAUL - THE JOURNEYS OF PAUL THE APOSTLE

The first persecutions

The priests of the temple thought that, with the death of Jesus, even his followers would be dispersed. Now they learn that the apostles preach in Jerusalem and teach the people: they announce the resurrection of Jesus and also the resurrection of those who believe in him. By now the number of Christians in Jerusalem is about five thousand.

One day, Peter and John are talking to the people when the guards sent by the priests of the temple arrive. The soldiers arrest the two apostles and lead them to the high priest. He questions them, but does not consider them dangerous; he orders them not to teach in the name of Jesus. But the apostles obey the Lord more than the high priest and continue in their preaching. Other arrests and other persecutions follow. But the priests of the temple cannot stop the path of the church. The followers of Jesus increase in

216

number every day. New communities flourish in Judea and throughout Palestine. The apostles, in order to devote themselves full-time to spreading the gospel, elect some men to take care of the poor, widows and orphans. Among them is Stephen, an ardent and full of zeal for the Lord.

The first martyr of the church

Stephen performs great wonders among the people. The priests of the temple fear that he overturns the religion and customs handed down by Moses. They have him arrested and questioned. Stephen, inspired by the Holy Spirit, says before the high priest: "God did not bind his presence to the temple of Jerusalem. The Highest does not live in buildings made by human hands. The sky is his throne and the earth the stool for his feet. Behold, I contemplate the heavens opened and Jesus is at the right hand of God. When the priests of the temple hear these words they grind their teeth in anger, then they break out in loud cries and they stop their ears so as not to hear any more. The crowd, stirred up by the priests, drags Stefano out of the city. Many, among the crowd, lay their cloaks at the feet of a young man from Tarsus in Cilicia, called Saul, and then begin to stone Stephen. While Stephen is struck by the stones thrown at him, he prays with his eyes turned to the sky: - Lord Jesus, welcome my spirit. Then bend your knees and shout out loud: - Lord, do not attribute e this sin to them. And saying these words Stephen dies. But the first bloodshed by a follower of Jesus is the seed of new Christians.

The conversion of Saul

Saul, at the foot of which Stephen's stoners had put down his cloaks to keep them, is a fervent Pharisee. He too is sincerely convinced that Christians are a danger to the religion of Moses. Saul approves of the killing of Stephen and rages against the church. He asks the priests of the temple for permission to persecute the followers of Jesus. Christian communities are multiplying. A thriving community is in the city of Damascus. Saul, with the authorization of the high priest, rides with an escort of soldiers towards Damascus to put the Christians of that city in chains.

And it happens that during the journey, suddenly, a dazzling light envelops Saul. He falls to the ground with his face in the dust. Ode a firm and sweet voice that tells him: - *Saul, Saul, why do you persecute me?* He answers: - *Who are you, oh Lord?* And the voice: - *I am Jesus, whom you persecute!* Suddenly Saul realizes he has got it all wrong. By persecuting the Christians, he was convinced in good faith to render a service to God, to the God of Abraham, of Isaac and of Jacob. Now, with his face in the dust, it is certain that Jesus is the Son of God, the Savior promised to the patriarchs and announced by the prophets. Saul is suddenly transformed into a new man by the grace of God. From persecutor, he becomes an ardent apostle. In Damascus, Saul is baptized.

The journeys of Paul the Apostle

Saul, called by the Roman name Paul, spends a period of prayer and reflection in the desert. Then he presents himself to the apostles in the Jerusalem community and receives from them the task of spreading the gospel to the pagan world. Paul becomes "the apostle of the Gentiles". Paul's long journeys to Turkey, Greece and Macedonia begin. During his apostolic journeys, Paul founded a community of Christians in Galatia and in the cities of Ephesus, Corinth, Philippi, Colossi. The Christians of these communities later send letters full of doctrine and passion. In them, he exposes the gospel that Jesus revealed to him, strengthens communities in faith, resolves doubts, warns, and corrects errors and deviations.

The letters attributed to Paul and contained in the New Testament are in all thirteen. During his travels, Paolo suffers persecution and faces hardships of all kinds. In the second letter to the Christians of Corinth, Paul summarizes the difficulties encountered and the sacrifices made to spread the gospel among the peoples.

"Five times I received thirty-nine whips from the Jews. Three times I was beaten with rods, once I was stoned and believed dead, three times I was shipwrecked. I spent a day and a night at the mercy of the waves. Countless journeys, the dangers of rivers, the dangers of brigands, dangers from my countrymen, dangers from the pagans, dangers in the cities, dangers in the desert, dangers on the sea, dangers from false brothers. Fatigue and labour, vigils without number, hunger and thirst, frequent fasting, cold and nakedness."

Despite these sufferings, Paul is in joy and for him now "to live in Christ and to die again". He glories himself on the cross of Christ "a scandal for the Jews, foolishness for the pagans, but for those who believe, the power and wisdom of God". Therefore - Paul writes to the Christians of Corinth - I am delighted in my infirmities, in the outrages, in the needs, in the persecutions, in the anguishes suffered for Christ. When I am weak, it is then that I am strong."

PART 3
PAUL TRAVELING TO ROME -
THE APOSTOLIC LETTERS -
THE APOCALYPSE

Paul traveling to Rome

Christianity is now widespread in almost the entire Roman Empire. In the very capital of the empire, Rome, there is a flourishing community of followers of Christ, founded by Peter. Paul ardently desires to visit the Christians of Rome. To them, he addresses a beautiful letter asking God to "open away" for him to visit them. The occasion arises when the priests of the temple and the leaders of the Jews accuse Paul before Porcius Festus, the Roman governor of Judea. Festus asks Paul and asks him: - Do you want to be judged before me in Jerusalem? Paolo, with his head, held high and with a proud look, replies: - I did not do any wrong to the Jews. If I'm guilty and I've committed something that deserves death, I don't refuse to die. But no one has the power to deliver me to the Jews. I appeal to Caesar.

Paul has Roman citizenship, so he has the right to be tried by a court in the capital of the empire. Porcius Festus replies to Paul: - *You have appealed to*

Caesar, to Caesar you will go. Paul's captive ship journey is fraught with danger. The ship that transports him to Rome is even shipwrecked on the island of Malta. But finally, Paolo arrives in Rome. There he remained under surveillance for two full years, waiting to be tried by Caesar's court. During that time he enjoys relative freedom and can welcome the Christians who come to him. "Announce to them the kingdom of God and teach the things concerning the Lord Jesus Christ, with all frankness and without impediment". With these words, the book of the Acts of the Apostles ends. According to tradition, Paul suffers martyrdom in the year 67AC , under the emperor Nero. Since he is a Roman citizen, his sentence is executed by beheading.

The apostolic letters

Almost all the other apostles testify to the gospel of Jesus with their blood. Peter suffered martyrdom in Rome around the year 64 AD. James, brother of John, is beheaded by order of Herod Agrippa in 44 AD. James, son of Alphaeus, was martyred in 62 AD. Peter, John, James of Alphaeus and Judas Thaddeus write letters to Christian communities. In these letters, which are part of the New Testament, the apostles urge Christians to observe above all the new commandment of Jesus: *the commandment of brotherly love.*

The Apocalypse

The last book of the New Testament, and therefore of the Bible, is called Apocalypse which means *"revelation."* The book is attributed to the apostle John and was written around 90 AD. The persecutions against Christians have now become more violent. The apostle John, with a difficult and rich language of symbols, announces however that the final victory will be of Christ. Evil, according to the promise made by God to Adam and Eve immediately after the sin of the origins, will be eradicated at the end of the world. The great dragon, the ancient serpent that seduces the earth, will be plunged into the abyss. Christ will reign and the followers of Christ will enter forever in the New Jerusalem, the city of God.

In the heavenly Jerusalem, according to the expression of the Apocalypse, "the servants of the Lord will see the face of God. There will be no more night and they will not have more need of the light of the lamp, neither of light of the sun, because the Lord God will illuminate them and they will reign in the ages of the centuries."

The Bible ends with a humble and ardent invocation addressed to the Lord so that the time for the definitive realization of salvation comes soon: Come, Lord Jesus! The grace of the Lord Jesus is with you all. Amen!

9 781801 231107